# Gustav Klimt

THE
GREAT
ARTISTS

# Gustav Klimt

## A N Hodge

ARCTURUS

ARCTURUS

This edition published in 2020 by Arcturus Publishing Limited
26/27 Bickels Yard, 151–153 Bermondsey Street,
London SE1 3HA

ISBN: 978-78828-568-1
AD006171UK

Printed in China

# CONTENTS

# INTRODUCTION

**G**ustav Klimt (1862–1918) occupies a unique position in the history of art. Born in Vienna towards the end of the nineteenth century, his art initially reflected the city's academic tradition. Before long, however, his paintings began to look like nothing the world had seen. Putting symbolism at the forefront of his work, Klimt created exotic, sensuous portrayals of women whose otherworldly demeanour recalled the art of ancient civilizations. Over time, he developed an elaborate technique using gold and silver leaf to decorate his paintings, often further ornamenting them with patterns and decorations drawn from an array of sources, including Byzantine mosaics and Egyptian murals.

Although Klimt's paintings became increasingly intricate and mysterious, the artist's own life was relatively straightforward. An introverted character, Klimt valued his privacy and lived modestly, mainly surrounded by family. In 1897, he found himself unwittingly thrust into the limelight as the leader of the Vienna Secession, a radical movement that saw value in all the arts while wanting to free art from the stifling confines of conservative, late nineteenth-century Vienna.

Alongside a desire to live a quiet life, Klimt was a man of few words who wrote very little other than a handful of postcards. The little that he has written has therefore been seized upon and pored over for clues, the obvious danger here being that people can easily read too much into what was intended as a fairly casual remark. Indeed, in one of his rare pronouncements, he talks about keeping his own life separate from his art, while tantalizingly suggesting that there were many pointers to be found in his paintings:

> There is nothing special about me. I am a painter who paints day after day from morning until night. Figures and landscapes, portraits less often.

> I have the gift of neither the spoken nor the written word, especially if I have to say something about myself or my work. Even when I have a simple letter to write I am filled with fear and trembling as though on the verge of being sea-sick. For this reason people must do without an artistic or literary self-portrait. And this should not be regretted. Whoever wants to know something about me – as an artist, the only notable thing – ought to look carefully at my pictures and try to see in them what I am and what I want to do. *

This hardworking, straightforward approach to his work is backed up by photographs that show an unremarkable stocky, bearded man dressed in a long robe and sandals. We know too that he loved routine, taking his breakfast at the same place, the Tivoli Café in Schönbrunn, every morning and seldom travelling anywhere, much less abroad. He never married, but had relationships with women who were often his models, and fathered a number of illegitimate children. His affairs were discreet and never appeared to ruffle any feathers. It is also clear that he defended his pictures fiercely when under attack and insisted on getting the price for them he believed he deserved.

It might seem surprising, perhaps even disappointing, that Klimt, given his unexceptional life, became the greatest artist of fin-de-siècle Vienna with an influence that stretches to this day. This book, part of *The Great Artists* series, explores the work of this intriguing and enigmatic Art Nouveau figure and attempts to unravel the many contradictions that lie at the heart of his complex, visionary paintings.

Forest Slope in Unterach on the Attersee, *1916. Working on an easel in the open air, Gustav Klimt painted many landscapes on the calm shores of Lake Attersee while on holiday with his companion Emilie Flöge.*

*from an undated statement, Vienna City Library

Founded in 1863, the Kunstgewerbeschule (the Vienna School of Arts and Crafts)
was set up to provide an advanced education for artists and designers. The building
now houses the University of Applied Arts.

# CHAPTER 1
# The Artist as a Young Man

**G**ustav Klimt was born in Baumgarten, a rural suburb of Vienna, on 14 July 1862. Although his family was by no means wealthy, they were artistic. His father, Ernst Klimt (1834–92), was a gold engraver by trade. Originally from a peasant family in Bohemia (now part of the Czech Republic), Ernst emigrated to Austria in search of work. Here he met and married a local Viennese girl Anna Finster (1836–1915) and the couple went on to have seven children – three boys and four girls. Anna originally had high hopes of becoming an opera singer, an ambition that stalled once she became a mother.

Despite working with rich metals, Ernst struggled to provide for his growing family, particularly after the Panic of 1873, a depression that began when the Vienna Stock Exchange crashed. Further tragedy hit the family a year later: when Klimt was 12, his five-year-old sister Anna died and not long afterwards his sister Klara had a mental breakdown. An hereditary predisposition towards mental illness was something that troubled Klimt throughout his life. For the time being, however, his family's ongoing financial struggle meant that he needed to focus his mind on turning his precocious talent for drawing to good use. He was encouraged to leave school at 14 to enter the Kunstgewerbeschule (the Vienna School of Arts and Crafts), the idea being that he might be able to contribute to the family finances by becoming an art teacher. Klimt was not the only one in the family to demonstrate an early artistic talent. His younger brothers Ernst and Georg Klimt also produced work that showed exceptional skills in art and design, and both would join their elder brother at the School of Arts and Crafts over the next couple of years.

Klimt studied at the Kunstgewerbeschule for seven years – from 1876 to 1883. Opened in 1864, it was a new institution modelled on London's Metropolitan School of Design, based in South Kensington (which would later become the Royal College of Art). The Principal, Professor Rudolf Eitelberger von Edelberg, was a reformer who looked to the English Arts and Crafts movement for inspiration. He saw all art forms as being of equal importance and believed that there should be no distinction between art and crafts – arguing that all the art forms should be brought together under the umbrella term *Gesamtkunstwerk*, or total artwork.

*Rudolf Eitelberger von Edelberg (1817–85) who founded the Kunstgewerbeschule.*

The education that Gustav received was traditional and thorough: he learnt the techniques of metalwork, mosaic and fresco and was exposed to work from different eras and cultures, including Greek and Egyptian art. Pupils at the School were encouraged to copy the work of other artists, to study perspective and refer to the classical model when constructing their drawings. Klimt was exceptionally talented at drawing and took this and decorative painting as his specialized subjects. Recognized as an exceptionally gifted student, Klimt was singled out to study under the prestigious painter Ferdinand Julius Laufberger (1829–81). The predominate influences on Klimt in these early years were Lawrence Alma-Tadema (1836–1912), the Dutch painter who settled in England and specialized in paintings of classical antiquity and Hans Makart (1840–84), a Viennese contemporary whose huge canvases evoking colourful, decorative historical scenes were much admired by Klimt. At this early stage there was very little to suggest that this model student would radically break free from the traditional, almost entirely academic approach for which he was so skilled – much less that he would be the initiator of a whole new artistic movement.

The Education of the Children of Clovis, *Lawrence Alma-Tadema, 1861. Klimt admired the Dutch painter for his draftsmanship and depictions of classical antiquity. In this work, Queen Clotilde, the wife of King Clovis, is shown training her three young children to hurl an axe to avenge the death of her father.*

Das Blinde Kuh Spiel, *Ferdinand Laufberger, 1865. Laufberger was appointed professor of figurative drawing and painting at the newly established Kunstgewerbeschule in 1868. In Laufberger's depiction of the children's game, the blind cow stumbles around trying to catch hold of its tormentors.*

In 1877 Gustav's brother, Ernst and their friend Franz von Matsch (1861–1942) also enrolled in the school. The two brothers and their friend shared a studio and began working together, and by 1880 they had started to receive commissions. A strong economy and Vienna's massive building boom, particularly on the Ringstrasse – the new boulevard constructed around the city – helped the three young artists and their fledgling business known as the Painters' Company (Künstler Compagnie) get plenty of paid work.

*Ferdinand Laufberger's students photographed in 1880. The professor sits to the left of Gustav and Ernst Klimt in the front row, with fellow company member Franz Matsch to the right at the back.*

In 1879 the three young artists – along with Klimt's younger brother Georg, who had also by now joined the School of Arts – were recommended by Prof Laufberger to work on decorations for *Festzug*, the pageant to celebrate the silver wedding celebrations of Emperor Franz Joseph to Elisabeth of Bavaria. Hans Makart, the painter most admired by Klimt and who was by now a leading celebrity in Viennese high society, was directing the work on the pageant. Known as the painter prince of Vienna, Makart had forged his own allegorical style based on classical antiquity, combining this with ornamental decoration and the swaggering manner of what came to be known as Late Baroque. Gustav greatly looked up to the older artist. Makart's work, whether as a painter or interior decorator, chiefly celebrated occasions and events in Viennese history. He worked on huge canvases that he treated rather like a stage set, filling them with lots of little people busily engaged in action. A confident and socially adept character, Makart used his studio as a salon, often re-enacting historical moments in costume, while going all out to impress members of Viennese high society.

Apart from admiring and assimilating aspects of Makart's glamorous allegorical style, Klimt particularly revered his use of rich, vibrant colour. Known as 'the magician of colours', Makart used to mix asphalt into his colours to make them more intense – combining this with a skilful use of light and shade to heighten the dramatic impact of his scenes. Klimt was completely overawed by Makart's talent – one story has it that he even bribed a servant to be allowed to sleep on the floor of his idol's studio in the hope that he might absorb some of his greatness.

After their work on the pageant, the three painters were employed in their own right in 1880 to create four decorative ceiling paintings for the Palais Sturany in Vienna – the magnificent residence of a Viennese architect. The two Klimt brothers and Matsch were still working in the Makart style – adapting his particular brand of classical antiquity – but for this commission they also took much inspiration from woodcuts created by the

*Entwurf zum Festzug, Hans Makart, 1879. Klimt's idol, Hans Makart, organized a festive procession to honour the 25th wedding anniversary of Emperor Franz Joseph I and Empress Elisabeth of Austria. This scroll-like painting is a record of the event that took place in Vienna in front of the imperial couple.*

great German fifteenth-century draughtsman Albrecht Dürer. Klimt studied these woodcuts assiduously and drew upon his own facility as an engraver (and what he had learned growing up with a master engraver as a father) to depict animals in his designs with extraordinary faithfulness. The next two years saw further work for the company in and out of Vienna, including commissions in Croatia and Bohemia (now the Czech Republic).

By the time the three artists left the School in 1883, the company was starting to flourish and they accepted further commissions to decorate villas and theatres outside Vienna, this time in Bucharest and Carlsbad. In 1884, Hans Makart died an early death at the age of 44. This must have been a difficult time for Klimt – a huge admirer of Makart's work, he had been literally following in his footsteps for several years. Nonetheless, it is a sign of how established Klimt and his fellow company members were by this time that the commissions continued to come in, and a year later they were working on new designs for the Emperor himself. Based on Shakespeare's *A Midsummer Night's Dream*, the scheme was for the Villa Hermes (known in German as the Hermesvilla), a country residence near Vienna, built by the Emperor Franz Joseph for his wife Sisi. Klimt's designs were well researched and well executed, but the Empress – who was 16 when she married Franz Joseph – became very timid over the years and refused to spend even a night there.

Schottenring 21, Detail in the Beletage, *Gustav Klimt and Franz von Matsch, 1888. In 1880 Klimt and Matsch took on a commission to develop work for the Palais Sturany.*

A Midsummer Night's Dream (Puck mistakes Lysander for Demetrius), *Gustav Klimt, Franz von Matsch and Ernst Klimt, 1884–5. From the Villa Hermes.*

# VIENNA AND THE *BELLE ÉPOQUE*

Towards the end of the nineteenth century, Austria was a country of contradictions and compromise. In 1867, after various military defeats and negotiations with Hungary, Emperor Franz Joseph was the figurehead of the Austro-Hungarian Empire. The Emperor ruled his dual monarchy from the magnificent Schönbrunn Palace in Vienna. In spite of a backdrop of military and political manoeuvring, this date marked the beginning of an unparalleled era of wealth and ostentation in Vienna known as the *Belle Époque*. With two million inhabitants between 1867 and World War I, Vienna stood alongside Paris as the impressive and resplendent capital of Europe.

Emperor Franz Joseph made some sweeping changes to the city's geography, including knocking down the city walls in 1857 to make way for the Ringstrasse, a horseshoe-shaped perimeter road. Many public buildings were erected, including a new parliament, museums, the Opera and the Court Theatre. Otto Wagner, an architect known for his modernist sympathies, designed the Stadtbahn, an urban rail network in 1890. Alongside the civic buildings, new private residences sprung up with ornate façades and lavishly decorated interiors. Drinking water was improved, and electric lamps and trams were introduced. This was a new world on the move – with a need to show that it was on the move.

In this febrile and pleasure-loving atmosphere, the dominant haute bourgeoisie flourished – hosting magnificent banquets and packing the theatres and opera houses. The poor, by contrast, remained poor and in inadequate housing.

The most significant impact of the *Belle Époque* was on the cultural life of the city. Amid all the opulence and decadence, the contrasts between old and new, traditional and modern became ever wider, driving the artists and intellectuals who were ensuring that Vienna was right at the heart of Europe's creative map. There was an astonishing array of musical talent centred around Vienna. Mozart, Haydn, Beethoven and Brahms had all lived and composed in the city. Now, Richard and Johann Strauss's waltzes and operettas were adopted with élan by the bourgeoisie for their lavish balls. Gustav Mahler lived in Vienna for 10 years, his work acting as a bridge between the nineteenth-century Austro-German tradition and the modernism of the early twentieth century. Initially, art and sculpture remained pretty much as it always had been – conservative, academic and based on rules and proportions – until Gustav Klimt and the Viennese Secession brought radical change.

The neurologist Sigmund Freud added to the new intellectual life of the city with his *Interpretation of Dreams*, published in 1899. Key to our understanding of psychoanalysis, the text built upon the analysis of Freud's own dreams and the personal crises surrounding the death of his father. His ideas about the power of the unconscious have played a central part in the way we view the self in the modern world, as well as the impact that the past has on the present.

With all the old certainties no longer providing the safe moral backdrop to the Habsburg Empire, Vienna experienced the *Belle Époque* as a golden age – a period of innovation and sheer aesthetic brilliance that Klimt helped to define and in which he was the brightest star. If Klimt's art, with its focus on the beautiful and the erotic, helped to establish the period's obsessions more than anyone else in Vienna at this time, it also helped to sow the seeds of its decay. The elegance and gaiety of Vienna in the late nineteenth century went through a process of turmoil and dissolution, coming to a shuddering end in 1914 with the outbreak of World War I.

Auditorium in the Old Burgtheater in Vienna, *1888. All the tiny figures in the audience in this gouache painting are actual portraits of Klimt's contemporaries, painted with astounding accuracy. One of Klimt's most celebrated early works, it won the Emperor's Prize in 1890.*

In 1886, the Painters' Company was given their most prestigious commission to date, to work on the interior of the Burgtheater, the replacement for the old theatre in Vienna. Up until this point the three painters had worked as a group, but important distinctions were beginning to emerge and now Klimt suddenly took the lead and found himself propelled into the limelight. The commission was to create 11 allegorical paintings in all. Klimt took on the largest and most demanding space – the vaulted entrance and the central ceiling. Appropriately, the motifs all came from theatrical productions, with Klimt working on scenes from a classical Greek drama, a medieval mystery play and Shakespeare's *Romeo and Juliet*. For this commission, Klimt started to draw upon realistic portraits using photographs as reference and his own family (including himself) as models. In 1888, Klimt received the Golden Cross of Honour from Emperor Franz Joseph for his contributions to the Burgtheater murals.

Some of the extraordinary realism that Klimt was to deploy in this commission can also be seen in *Auditorium in the Old Burgtheater* (see p. 15), a separate painting he made in 1888. This gouache painting of the old Burgtheater before it was destroyed unexpectedly reveals the view of the auditorium as seen from the stage. The audience is represented in astounding detail – all the 200 tiny portraits are faithfully accurate, and individual personalities including the composer Brahms are recognizable, as well as contemporary politicians and dignitaries. This ability to conjure up such an extraordinary illusion through such careful attention to truth – presenting the viewer with a heightened version of reality – is one of the hallmarks of Klimt's later style and one at which he was to prove a supreme master.

Klimt's ambitious painting did not go unnoticed or unrewarded. Indeed, fashionable Viennese

society members depicted in it were more than happy to have been modelled and celebrated in this way. *Auditorium in the Old Burgtheater* won the Emperor's Prize in 1890, for which Klimt received 400 guilders.

If Klimt began his professional career painting interior murals and ceilings in large public buildings, he was also pursuing other projects, including several portrait commissions. Most often painted from photographs, these included the portrait of *Joseph Pembaur*, the pianist and piano teacher, 1890, notable for its hyperrealism and decorative broad frame. Klimt had also created designs for a publication entitled *Allegories and Emblems* for the Viennese publisher Martin Gerlach while he was still at art school in 1881. The book was designed to instruct students on how to depict allegorical themes, and Klimt worked on a series of designs that showed his evolving style. One significant device was Klimt's use of a broad frame, sometimes in gold, as a border for his classical figures, with decorative details that echoed the content of the main image.

*Joseph Pembaur, 1890. Born in Innsbruck in 1875, Pembaur was a piano teacher and concert pianist. Klimt's near photographic portrait shows his great skill as a realist painter.*

Egyptian Art I and II, Greek Antiquity I and II, *1890–1. The Kunsthistorisches Museum in Vienna opened in 1891 under Emperor Franz Joseph who commissioned a cycle of paintings by Klimt for the main staircase. These early works reveal the beginning of Klimt's Art Nouveau style.*

In 1890 the Painter's Company secured another hugely significant commission, to work on the newly built Kunsthistorisches (Museum of Art History) in Vienna. Hans Makart was originally proposed for the commission, but it was given to Klimt and his company after his death. The building was the home of the Emperor's art collection and was to be open to the public for the first time. Although the artists were informed that their designs had to pay homage to their benefactor and his magnificent patronage of the arts, they produced a comprehensive, eclectic scheme that ranged over many different periods and styles of art history.

On this commission, Klimt began to make innovations that not only made him stand apart from the work of his fellow artists but which surpassed any of his own advances to date. His decorations plucked ideas and inspiration from the ancient civilizations of Greece and Egypt, mixing these with references to the work of the artists of the Italian Renaissance artists, such as Bellini, Botticelli and Donatello. Aside from taking the viewer on a chronological romp through the history of art, Klimt created wondrous illusions – his painted figures on the ceilings and walls look literally like they have been carved out of stone. Among these illusionistic portrayals, *Ancient Greece (The girl from Tanagra)* stood out. This young woman is not merely a representation of that idealized classical beauty already familiar to Viennese society – she has the look of a contemporary woman. She has a pre-Raphaelite head of hair and a languid, sensuous look, foreshadowing the femmes fatales beauties that were to become the trademark of Klimt's mature work.

Love, 1895. *In this romantic allegorical image, Klimt depicts a young couple wrapped in each other's arms and shrouded in mist. Above their heads, harbingers of death and sickness hover. The roses on each of the golden panels signify the fragility of youth and beauty.*

In 1891, Klimt became a member of the co-operative Austrian Artists' Society, a powerful and conservative group representing all that was traditional about Viennese art. Success meant that the Painter's Company could move to a larger studio in the Josefstadt area of Vienna; success that was hugely overshadowed by the deaths of his father and his brother Ernst the following year. Gustav took on the financial responsibility for his brother's widow and child as well as his mother and younger siblings. Grief affected Klimt's artistic vision and he painted little for four years. However, he eventually emerged with a new confidence about his evolving personal style, which was to take him even further away from his contemporaries.

Matsch was a conformist when it came to art, wanting to work in a traditional style with appropriate and time-honoured subject matter. He moved out of the Josefstadt studio, though the pair continued to work together on commissions, including one received in 1894, to complete four decorative panels and the large ceiling in the Great Hall of the University of Vienna. The concept for the work was the triumph of light over darkness, the four panels representing Theology, Philosophy, Medicine and Jurisprudence. The paintings took Klimt nine years to complete, during which time he crossed swords with both Matsch and the commissioners on several occasions. Essentially, Klimt's new evolving symbolist style was at variance with the cultural expectations of traditional bourgeois society. His critics objected to the content of the work – the nudity and the lack of moral purpose – as well as what they considered to be the baffling symbolism.

Klimt's evolving allegorical style can also be seen in *Love* and *Music I*, two portfolios of works sent to the publisher Martin Gerlach in 1895. Gerlach approached Klimt for paintings for a book entitled *Allegories and Emblems*, which would provide artists with ideas and models when depicting allegorical themes. In *Love* a man and a woman are clasped in a romantic embrace. It is subject matter that Klimt would return to several times, most notably in *The Kiss*, 1907. Here, it is almost as if time has stopped still. The golden border traps the couple in a cubicle, forcing their bodies closer together. They appear as in a dream, shrouded in mist, with faces representing their tragic destiny hovering above. The surrounding golden, stylized background was to become one of Klimt's trademarks from this point on, the frame picking up on the decorative details on the inner canvas. *Music I* shows a young woman, in a deep blue dress, with a cloud of auburn hair against a backdrop of classical statuary. Lost in thought, she plucks at her golden lute. Again, the excess of rich gold decoration and the stylized, non-naturalistic way Klimt uses it across the canvas, is a harbinger of what was to come.

Music I, *1895. A painting that shows Klimt's early ability to draw from different sources to create a harmonious whole. Standing against a classical setting, the young woman herself seems drawn from more modern times.*

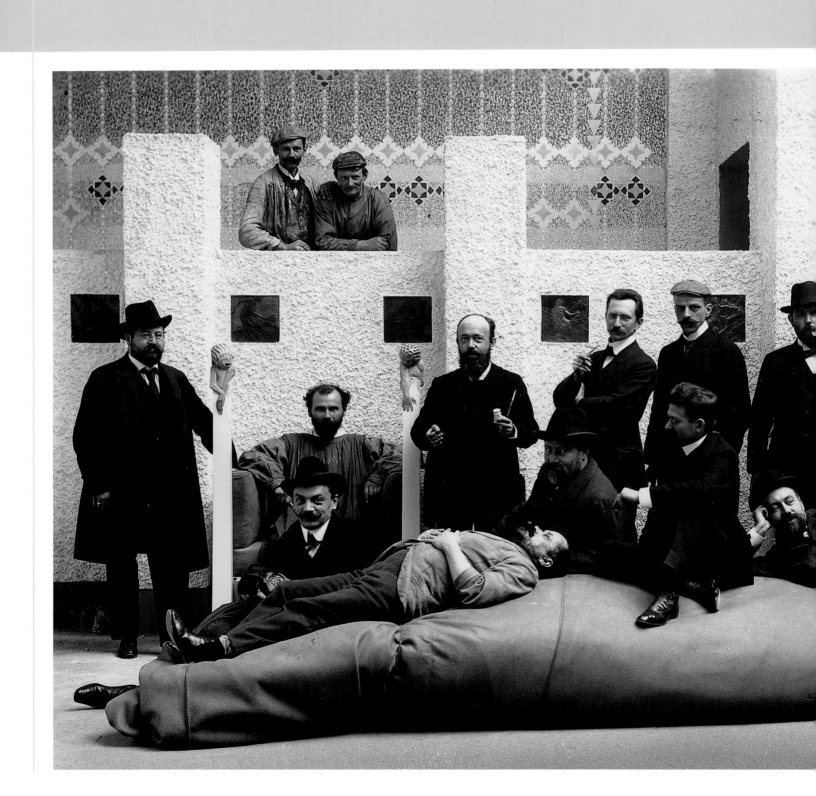

# CHAPTER 2
# The Secession Years

A ustria in the 1890s was something of an artistic backwater. There were important changes happening in the arts in the rest of Europe, not least in France, where the entirely original Impressionist paintings of Manet and Degas were starting to find a wider audience. In Vienna, housed in a large mansion off the city's Ringstrasse, the Austrian Artists' Society had been founded in 1861 and represented all that was traditional, bourgeois and inward-looking about the cultural life of the city. Promoting Austrian artists at the expense of all others, the society staged exhibitions that Klimt and others felt were dull, lacking in 'modern' work from abroad and unashamedly commercial. It was against this backdrop that the Viennese Secession was founded in 1897, essentially as a form of protest against the established art of the time in Vienna. (*Secession* is a term most often used when part of a state breaks away and achieves its own autonomy.)

If the impetus behind a new movement was a desire for change and to embrace some of the exciting and progressive developments abroad, this was also fuelled by the success of a counterpart breakaway movement in Munich. Initially seen as a separate group under the wing of the Austrian Artists' Society, it soon became clear to the malcontents that their position within the parent organization was untenable. A formal constitution was drawn up and Klimt was elected the first President of the new Union of Austrian Artists (Secession).

Although by all accounts quite shy and introverted, Klimt suddenly found himself propelled into the spotlight. He was clearly passionate about the need to reinvigorate artistic life in Vienna because he had personally experienced many frustrations and disappointments on commissions. However, his unhappy and at times depressive temperament made him an unlikely spearhead for a revolutionary movement.

In breaking away from the establishment, the artists of the Viennese

*A group of artists involved in the 14th Secession exhibition of 1902. Klimt is seated on a chair in the second row, dressed in his characteristic smock type robe. Koloman Moser, his friend and fellow Secessionist, is in front of him.*

Secession did not have a manifesto or even a particular style of art and design that they favoured. From the start they welcomed international artists, inviting leading Czech and German artists to join. The first exhibition staged in the summer of 1898 was predominantly drawn from the work of international artists.

One founding principle of the Secession, and one which was ultimately to play an important part in its demise, was a belief that all the various art forms should be on an equal footing. Architecture and design were seen as sharing centre stage with painting and sculpture – fuelled in part by the fact that architect Josef Hoffman and graphic designer Koloman Moser were leading figures in the new movement.

The Secession also founded their own journal, which set new standards in typography and graphic design. *Ver Sacrum* (*Sacred Spring*) was published in a square format and showcased the new Secessionist style with its lyrical and decorative imagery. Klimt was a regular contributor for two years. In the first issue, his bold line drawing *Nuda Veritas* showed a naked femme fatale staring directly at the viewer – a drawing he was to develop into a painting in 1899, oil and gold on canvas and 2 metres (6½ feet) high.

*The two Secession artists who went on to found the Wiener Werkstätte. On the left, Austrian architect and designer Josef Hoffmann (1870–1956) and on the right, artist Koloman Moser (1868–1918).*

*Poster for the First Art Exhibition of the Secession Movement, 1898.
The Secessionists were keen to make their exhibitions stand out from
everything that had gone before. Klimt's modern design, with its image
of Theseus fighting the Minotaur, uses blank space and decorative type to
create a distinctive image.*

The journal developed a new harmony between word and image. Writing was an important part of the magazine and the Bohemian-Austrian poet Rainer Maria Rilke and English playwright and poet Charles Swinburne both contributed to it. In the journal, and in their work in general, the Secessionists paid special attention to literature, often quoting from prose and poetry. As for Klimt himself, he was always mindful of his literary heritage, and allegedly used to carry books around with him, texts such as *Faust* by Goethe and *The Divine Comedy* by Dante. He produced several covers for the journal, which quickly became collector's items.

Klimt, with architect Hoffman and fellow painter Carl Moll, were the main drivers behind the Secession's exhibitions. Klimt designed the poster for their first Vienna Secession exhibition in March 1898. Inspired by ancient Greek vases, the top third of the image features Theseus fighting the Minotaur and shows the sinewy body of a young naked man (Theseus appears without the customary fig leaf) driving a sword into the Minotaur. Richly symbolic, Klimt portrays the young man's struggle as a battle between the forces of light and dark. The design has a modern fresh feel with one third of the image left blank and the bottom quarter spelling out the details of the exhibition in an elegant script decorated with spirals and dots.

The Secession's first exhibition opened in a space hired from the government – to great acclaim. It attracted nearly 60,000 visitors, some good reviews and, importantly, sales that meant money could be ploughed back into the project to build a new pavilion for successive exhibitions. Klimt's friend and colleague Hoffman and another architect Joseph Maria Olbrich worked on the new building, which opened in record time for the Second Secessionist exhibition in November 1898. Significantly, the forward-thinking motto over the doorway declared: 'To our time its art, and to art its freedom'.

Pallas Athene, *1898. The Secessionists adopted Pallas Athene – the goddess who was the patron of arts and crafts – as their emblem. Her burnished gold armour and helmet point the way forward to Klimt's excessive use of gold in his later portraits.*

The Emperor himself visited the second exhibition, which again attracted record numbers of visitors and substantial sales. Klimt showed seven works this time, including his portrayal of *Pallas Athene*, the Greek goddess of Wisdom, Crafts and War. In this painting, Klimt portrays a woman warrior standing erect with a long gold spear or orb and a magnificent golden headdress and breastplate. Her eyes are glacial, her expression fixed and determined. There is no doubt that she is or will be victorious, her triumph being over her (most likely) male adversaries or perhaps even men in general. In her right hand, Athene holds a tiny figure of a naked woman – frail, fleshy, yet protected by her goddess.

Klimt was following standard themes in tackling the battle of the sexes, but his Athene resembles a more modern and intimidating woman, rather than the standard goddesses seen in classical paintings. The painting is an amalgamation of several styles and influences that Klimt has made all his own. There is a new level of golden embellishment and ornament – his brother Georg made the decorative frame – and this marks the beginning of Klimt's blurring of the boundaries between flesh and gold ornamentation, with flesh becoming gold and gold becoming flesh.

*Pallas Athene* also marked the beginning of Klimt's love affair with strong women protagonists. Although the female form was crucially important to Art Nouveau, Klimt continued to portray his female heroines as assertive and in charge of their own destinies, which was at odds with traditional representations of women as meek and acquiescent.

In 1898, alongside all his Secessionist activity, Klimt also took on another commission – the decorations for the Ringstrasse mansion of Nikolaus Dumba. Klimt researched and executed two works for the music room – *Music II* and *Schubert at the Piano*, which reveal a new softness and approach to light, helping to bridge the gap between his early classical academic style and his later symbolist inspired work. The heroine in *Music II* has all the hallmarks of a later Klimt femme fatale – the bouffant hair, the winsome appearance and the detached languid air. *Schubert at the Piano* is a soft, flattering portrait of the bourgeoisie's favourite musical composer, shown playing to a group of society ladies in a candlelit setting.

In the same year Klimt painted *Sonja Knips*, the first of his portraits of Viennese society wives. Patronage was extremely important to the fledgling Secession movement and most patrons came from the Jewish families of the Viennese bourgeoisie. These included the steel magnate Karl Wittgenstein, the Lederer family and the Knips family, who had made their money in metal industry and banking and had already engaged Josef Hoffman to design their house.

*Schubert at the Piano, 1899. Klimt painted this portrait of Schubert for one of his patrons, the Greek industrialist Nikolaus Dumba. The softness and light as well as the stippled brushstrokes lend it an Impressionist quality.*

Sonja Knips, *1898. Sonja, the wife of Anton Knips, another of Klimt's patrons, is seated in a gauzy pink dress, and set against a plain dark background. The softness of the portrait recalls some of those by Whistler whom Klimt knew through reproductions of his work.*

Medicine, 1907. *This detail from* Medicine, *one of the notorious University paintings, shows Hygeia, the Greek goddess of health, with a snake wound round her arm and holding a cup. Looking upwards, Klimt's use of perspective emphasizes her extraordinary strength.*

Klimt's portrait of Sonja was to grace the Knips' salon. It is a work that shows a number of different influences, including Klimt's old master Makart, in terms of the off-centre, sideways composition, and the American painter J M Whistler in terms of the softness, in particular the feathery pink brushstrokes Klimt has used on her dress. Klimt never met Whistler (who was primarily based in England), but they corresponded and he saw reproductions of Whistler's work in art gazettes such as *The Studio* and *The Art Journal*. Klimt greatly admired Whistler in terms of composition, colouring and technique. In this portrait, Sonja Knips has a poised, proud, perhaps even disdainful expression that Klimt was starting to make his own in his ongoing portraits of femmes fatales.

Rows over the ceiling paintings, commissioned in 1894 by the Ministry of Education for the Great Hall of the University of Vienna, continued to dog Klimt over the next decade. The theme for the work – the victory of the intellect over ignorance – seemed especially ironic since Klimt had to fight prejudice and incomprehension from a multitude of people, including members of the university, academics, the clergy and even Matsch, his fellow artist and business partner.

Unsurprisingly, given all the disagreements, the paintings remained unfinished for many years. However, in 1900, Klimt decided to show the incomplete *Philosophy* to members of the university, who were unanimous in their criticism of it. This was in part due to the inclusion of naked figures and their unexplained links to philosophy as well as to Klimt's inexplicable symbolism. This did not deter Klimt from sending the painting to the 1900 World Exhibition in Paris, where it was awarded a gold medal.

# THE BEETHOVEN FRIEZE

Klimt and his fellow Secessionists saw the 14th exhibition at their building in Vienna in 1902 as special and they wanted people to experience a total work of art. They decided to celebrate Beethoven, whose work was greatly admired at the time. An heroic sculpture of Beethoven by Max Klinger, the German symbolist artist, formed the centrepiece. Music was arranged for the occasion – the fourth movement of Beethoven's *Ninth* was performed at the opening with an orchestra conducted by Gustav Mahler. Work by various artists selected in relation to the theme was positioned in the many spaces around the building. Klimt agreed to provide a mural.

Architect Josef Hoffman created a new interior out of bare, concrete – pale walls, forming an ideal backdrop to Klimt's delicate golden visions. Situated for the most part high up on the walls, Klimt painted directly onto the dry plaster, applying a range of decorative materials, including silver and gold leaf, mirror, coloured glass, chalk, graphite and even curtain rings.

Klimt saw his frieze as a symbolic translation of Beethoven's last symphony, in which the central theme was the life cycle. Symbolic figures suggested the passage of time from procreation, pregnancy and birth to disease, old age and death. At 34 metres (112 feet) long, the *Beethoven*

The Beethoven Frieze, *(detail: The Hostile Forces), 1902. Klimt's tribute to Beethoven created for the Secession Building in Vienna, hit a sour note with this depiction of the Hostile Forces. The giant ape Typhoeus was perceived to be particularly hideous as were the three Gorgons – Disease, Madness and Death.*

*Frieze* comprised three painted walls in a sequence. Essentially the three parts depicted firstly the suffering of the weak and a yearning for happiness; secondly hostile forces; and finally, the redemptive power of the arts.

It was the second part of the Frieze dedicated to *Hostile Forces* with its three Gorgons – disease, madness, death – that created the most negative reaction from Klimt's contemporaries. The image of the naked older woman in the foreground with her large breasts and stomach led to charges of ugliness and even obscenity. The frightening apparition of a giant ape, complete with a serpent's tail and wing, visible despite the wealth of ornamental detail, further alienated an audience already uncomfortable with images of skeletal figures with protruding eyes. Aside from the criticism for the rigidity and repulsive nature of his figures, Klimt's contemporary audience was particularly repelled by the male and female nudes. His wide range of erotic vocabulary was just far too challenging for his viewers.

The final section, *The Arts, Chorus of Paradise*, is an altogether more uplifting image, in which a choir of girls sings Beethoven's 'Ode to Joy'. A naked couple in the foreground appears to be enjoying a moment of sexual intimacy. Like so many of Klimt's allegorical works – and despite further explanations in the catalogue that was produced at the time – much of the exact meaning remains unclear. Nevertheless, with its further entanglement of Klimt's erotic and aesthetic sensibilities, the *Beethoven Frieze* was and still is considered an important milestone in his career. Rescued from the walls and kept in storage, the work was preserved and finally put back on show in 1986.

Klimt showed *Medicine* the following year, and again the reaction was nothing short of disastrous. This time it was physicians pitching in to condemn the fact that the work did not do enough to celebrate medical and scientific advances. The central image of Hygeia, the goddess of health, was seen as another of Klimt's femme fatales – with her arms encircled by golden snakes suggestive more of a sorceress than a spiritual being of enlightenment. The work was deemed to be inappropriate, depressing and mocking in equal measure.

Undeterred, Klimt applied for the position of professor at the Academy of Fine Arts (a position he had applied for in 1893) but was turned down. It was his last application for a teaching position. In 1903 he also travelled to Ravenna in Italy and was greatly affected by the Byzantine mosaics that he saw there.

The Secession, meanwhile, continued to stage more than one exhibition a year – between 1898 and 1905 they organized a total of 23 exhibitions. Arnold Böcklin, Edvard Munch, Henri de Toulouse–Lautrec, Auguste Rodin, Alphonse Mucha, Walter Crane and Charles Rennie Mackintosh were among the international artists who showed regularly.

In 1902, Klimt contributed a three-part frieze to the 14th exhibition. Known as the *Beethoven Frieze*, Klimt's work was designed to accompany a special orchestration by Gustav Mahler of the fourth movement of Beethoven's *Ninth Symphony* to be performed at the opening. Klimt applied his utopian vision to three painted walls in sequence. His focus was the optimistic idea of the salvation of mankind through the power of art and love. Rich in ornamentation and suffused with gold, mosaic patterning and brilliant colour, Klimt's complex and powerful work drew upon a range of different styles and references, including Greek vase painting, Egyptian painting, African sculpture and Japanese prints.

The *Beethoven Frieze* divided its audience. Although much admired for its ambitious lyricism,

the symbolism of the work continued to baffle some of its viewers, while others were disturbed by its frank, unabashed portrayal of sexuality – in particular the plethora of nude figures, mostly female but some male. Others were more positive in their response, including the artist Auguste Rodin, who exhibited at the first Secessionist exhibition in Vienna and who congratulated Klimt on his 'so tragic and so divine work'.

In 1903, the Secession movement spawned

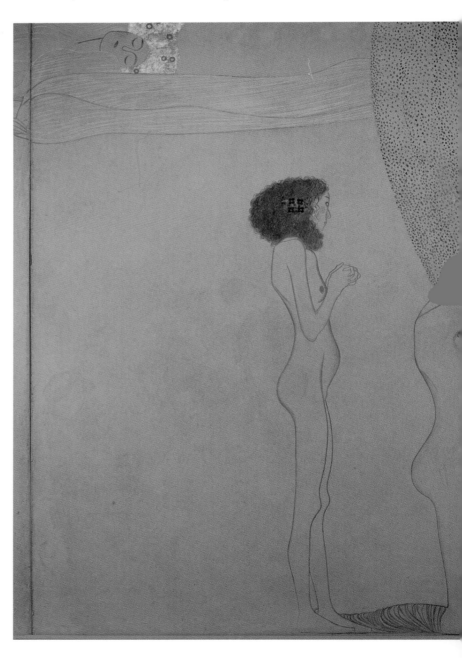

another vital offshoot – namely the Wiener Werkstätte, or Vienna Workshop. Brought together by the architect Josef Hoffman and the designer Koloman Moser, the idea behind this powerful grouping of artists and designers was to create a cooperative that would sell work, train young artists and actively promote the work of all its artist/designer members on an equal footing. Klimt had close ties with the fledgling set-up and designed furniture and textiles for them. It also brought him into closer contact with the woman who was to become his greatest friend and companion, Emilie Flöge.

The Beethoven Frieze, *(detail:* Yearning for Happiness), 1902. *In the first part of the* Beethoven Frieze, *Klimt depicted the sufferings of feeble mankind. The well-armed strong one in golden armour is being impelled to take up the struggle for happiness.*

# EMILIE FLÖGE

If 1897 denotes the founding of the Viennese Secession, it also marks the year that Gustav Klimt first started spending summers with his companion Emilie Flöge in the Kammer am Attersee region of Upper Austria.

After his father and brother had died in 1892, Gustav Klimt assumed guardianship of Helene Flöge, his brother's widow and baby daughter, and through this became friendly with her younger sister Emilie, who was 12 years his junior (and then aged

*Emilie Flöge on holiday in Lake Attersee c. 1910. She is wearing a white gown with a textured frontispiece designed by Klimt.*

*Emilie Flöge wears a dress designed by Klimt for her fashion house – a characteristic Secessionist design with contrasting black and white stripes and incorporating a chequerboard pattern.*

only 18). Emilie's father was a master craftsman who manufactured smoking pipes and she was the youngest of four siblings, with two sisters, Pauline and Helene, and a brother, Hermann. In 1895, Pauline opened a dressmaking school, where Emilie gained couture knowledge and skills, paving the way for the opening of a new designer clothing business a decade later with her sister Helene.

In 1903, the Wiener Werkstätte, or Vienna Workshop, was set up as a co-operative for artists and designers. Based on the English Arts and Crafts movement, the aim was to get rid of hierarchical distinctions between art and craft while promoting the specialist nature of all the arts. Both Klimt and Emilie were involved with the Werkstätte, and in 1904 founder members Josef Hoffman and Klaus Moser helped to refit the interior of the Flöge Sisters fashion house in one of Vienna's most prestigious streets. Klimt, meanwhile, designed some new fabrics for the sisters – featuring bold colours and striking patterns. Flöge and the salon were supporters of 'reform clothing' in Vienna, a liberating style of clothing for women based on free-flowing dresses and an end to the tight-fitting corset.

A photograph of Klimt and Flöge shows two people caught in a pose that looks almost like the precursor to a dance. She is smiling at the camera, wearing a voluminous, tent-like dress made of material designed by Klimt and featuring a black and white chessboard pattern and stripes; the artist wears a floor-length painter's smock. There are several similar photos showing the pair in long kaftans, posing in a boat on Lake Attersee where, for three months most summers until 1916, they made regular excursions together.

The relationship between Klimt and Emilie seems mainly to have revolved around a deep and lasting friendship. From the time they met, they were close companions who not only holidayed together but went to the opera and theatre and attempted to learn French. Whether they were ever lovers is a matter of speculation – they never married and Klimt pursued many other sexual affairs while they were seeing each other. Most of his lovers were very different from the smart, independent, talented, middle-class Emilie Flöge – she represented a very pure and sacred kind of love at odds with the many models and working-class women with whom he actually had sexual relations. It has also been speculated that Flöge, who never married and had no other known partners, was a lesbian. This is one explanation for the intense friendship and creative partnership she maintained with Klimt, who happily indulged his avid sexual appetite elsewhere but clearly preferred her company above all others.

A Theatrical Buffoon on a Makeshift Stage at Rothenburg, 1893. *Klimt's brother Ernst originally painted this work on the Burgtheater ceiling in 1893. Klimt finished it after his brother's death, and in the centre added a portrait of a young Emilie Flöge in a red and green gown.*

Klimt used Emilie as a model several times. In 1891, when she was only 17, he painted her portrait. Her face is in profile and the painting has an integral gold frame decorated with Japanese style foliage. In this, Flöge's serious expression and determined gaze indicates a strong-willed temperament somewhat at odds with the youthful innocence of her gauzy white gown. A youthful Flöge also appeared in a painting called *A Theatrical Buffoon on a Makeshift Stage at Rothenburg*. This was originally painted on the Burgtheater ceiling in 1893 by his brother Ernst, and Klimt finished the work after his brother's death, adding a portrait of Emilie standing in a red and green gown.

A later portrait from 1902 shows Flöge again, this time wearing one of Klimt's designs for her fashion house – a floor-length blue dress with a large elliptical shape of the same fabric behind her head, framing her face and curly hair. The stunning dress has an all-over pattern of gold and silver circles and bars – Flöge is presented as a bejewelled icon, an idealized portrait in which her goddess-like status and modesty is literally preserved in a golden casing. Hand on hip, Flöge radiates self-possession, her sangfroid seemingly offering a direct challenge to the viewer. Interestingly, this is not a portrait that she, her family or Klimt himself much liked and he sold it a few years later to the City Museum in Vienna.

Some claim that Emilie was the model for the woman depicted in *The Kiss*. The evidence for this is scant, however, and seems to be based on wish fulfillment by those who want to see Flöge and Klimt's relationship as more than platonic.

At the end of World War II, Flöge's possessions, including clothing from her business and gifts from Klimt, were destroyed in a house fire at her home on Ungargasse, where she had been forced to relocate her business following the annexation of Austria into Nazi Germany in 1938. She died aged 78 in 1952 in Vienna.

*Fraulein Emilie Flöge, 1902. Klimt's portrait of his companion Emilie Flöge. Klimt borrowed the two signature boxes on the right at the bottom from Japanese art – one of his great passions.*

## WIENER WERKSTÄTTE

The Wiener Werkstätte, the cooperative of artists and designers formed in 1903, was the brainchild of two important Secession members – the architect Josef Hoffman and the designer Koloman Moser – and their financial backer, the wealthy textile manufacturer and patron of Klimt, Fritz Waerndorfer. The concept behind the new set-up followed on from the earlier idea of *Gesamtkunstwerk*, or total artwork, espoused by the Secession. Any hierarchy between art forms should be disregarded. Art and design were considered of equal importance. Makers should produce objects that were at once aesthetically pleasing, simple and functional. Harmony was the key word when it came to design. Nothing was considered off-limits or unworthy of a design make over. Grand architectural projects – the complete overhaul of a Viennese mansion, for example – was a project to be tackled alongside the redesign of pots, pans, textiles, clothes and jewellery.

The Werkstätte's egalitarian principles and practical, hands-on emphasis was inspired by the English Arts and Craft movement, following on from William Morris, John Ruskin and the work of Charles Rennie Mackintosh. All three founder members were particularly enthused by Mackintosh, whose work had been shown at the eighth Secession exhibition in 1900. They were drawn to the way his work created a subtle fusion between geometric lines and angles and the sweeping curves of symbolism. They also much admired the fact that Mackintosh and his wife Margaret Macdonald created entire rooms filled with beautiful objects.

The entrance of the Wiener Werkstätte's shop in the inner city of Vienna, c. 1907.

The idea behind the Werkstätte was to create a level playing field for art and design. This depended on investing time and energy into specialist techniques, particularly as it was believed that some of these were threatened by a move towards industrialization. Workshops were set up to train younger artists in metalwork, furniture, bookbinding and glassmaking, for example.

After the success of the workshops, and with about a hundred people working there, Hoffman and Moser felt that the applied arts needed more of a showcase, and set about finding new premises. In 1905, they found a new home in Vienna at 32/34 Neustiftgasse, where a high-ceilinged reception area and exhibition room could display many of the objects made by the Werkstätte members. Aside from producing a wide range of items for sale, many of the members also contributed to the architectural commissions that Hoffman received.

One project that Hoffman worked on was to design a sanatorium at Purkersdorf to the west of Vienna. His sketches for the building show a spare, uncluttered concrete building with little ornamentation, typifying the Werkstätte's pure, restrained yet graceful approach to design. *Fruit Basket*, 1904, made by Hoffman, is another typical 'pure' piece of design: all in silver, the basket consists of a tray standing on thin

*The exterior of Palais Stoclet designed by Josef Hoffman for Belgian industrialist Adolphe Stoclet on the outskirts of Brussels. A great masterpiece of Art Nouveau design.*

geometric bars, decorated with tiny beads of silver. Overall it is a very elegant design, that typifies the Wiener Werkstätte's approach to elevating functional objects.

The exact moment that Klimt, a board member and close associate of all three founder members, began to become closely involved with the Wiener Werkstätte is not known. Having once declared that it is 'better to spend one day on one thing than to produce ten things in one day', Klimt recognized that his considered approach to his craft was a natural fit with the group. There were many points of contact. The Wiener Werkstätte often made frames for Klimt's paintings. This was not a simple case of choosing the right frame, since Klimt saw his frames as an extension of the picture itself and integral to the overall effect of the work. Klimt also had his studio redesigned by members of the Werkstätte, early on in the group's existence. Klimt was not initially best pleased with the result as he was away when it was realized, leaving him with several hefty items of furniture, including a Hoffman-designed sideboard that he was forced to navigate around in his studio. Klimt also bought several items from the Werkstätte, including jewellery and ceiling lights.

Klimt's collaborations with the Werkstätte extended to painting pictures for interiors, as well as designing fabrics and clothes. Along with Moser and Hoffman, Klimt helped to redesign the interior of the Flöge Fashion house, creating a new stylish showroom for the Flöge sisters. In return, the three sisters – Helene, Emilie and Pauline – often featured the Werkstätte's stark geometric fabric designs in their shop.

Koloman Moser left the group after disagreements with Waerndorfer in 1907. His departure marked the beginning of a new ornamental phase in the group's development, with Hoffman introducing luxurious materials into his architectural projects. Hoffman designed the grand building Palais Stoclet for Belgian industrialist Adolphe Stoclet on the outskirts of Brussels. Hoffman employed a team of craftsmen from the Werkstätte, working on every last detail in the house, from the doorknobs to the cutlery. Hoffman also asked Klimt to create a mosaic frieze for the ground floor. This frieze drew on a vast array of ornamental items and sumptuous materials, heralding the group's new style, which Waerndorfer did much to encourage. One of Klimt's most important patrons, Waerndorfer was the driving force behind another of the later projects involving Hoffman, Klimt and other Werkstätte members – namely, the design and decoration of Cabaret Fledermaus, a Viennese nightclub.

# THE STOCLET FRIEZE

In 1905, the Belgian financier Adolph Stoclet commissioned Josef Hoffman and the Wiener Werkstätte to complete their dream of creating a total of work of art – namely, an entire new house and all its contents. No ceiling was put on the budget. Klimt's role was again to provide a mural – in this case, a frieze that ran along two sides of the rectangular dining room, with an accompanying panel on the short wall.

This commission lasted for four years and Klimt did extensive preliminary work. He drew preparatory cartoons and, in collaboration with the makers in the Wiener Werkstätte who engraved the designs into the marble, reapplied the outlines by hand. His designs draw upon the Byzantine mosaics of Ravenna and Oriental art. The Tree of Life is the work's central motif. The golden branches of the trees spiral over the entire wall and contain a host of tiny elements, including birds, flowers and Egyptian-style eyes. In *The Expectation*, an inlaid panel, a gorgeously bejewelled Egyptian queen wrought out of rich gold triangles waves her arms and sidesteps. In *The Embrace* the tip of a man's

*Palais Stoclet's ornate marble dining room showing Klimt's frieze.*

head is barely visible seen from behind as he is swallowed up in an embrace with his lover. Both figures are covered in richly decorated cloaks. The work echoes the placing of the couple in the last section of the *Beethoven Frieze* and prefigures Klimt's celebrated painting *The Kiss*, produced only a couple of years later.

The *Stoclet Frieze* is the most abstract of the two murals. As decoration it is sumptuous and makes the most of its costly materials. As a piece of work designed for a private residence, it was intended to please the eye rather than make a grand allegorical statement. Still hurt by the reception he had received for his earlier mural, Klimt was reluctant to let the Viennese public in to see the work. The Palais Stoclet still exists although nowadays in a different form. The frieze he created for it was the last of Klimt's mural works.

The Tree of Life, Stoclet Frieze, 1905–09. *The central image of the Frieze, Klimt's theme is the Garden of Eden with its allusions to nature, the seasons and the abundance of life.*

The contradiction that became more painfully obvious in the later years of the Werkstätte was that despite its desire to be an egalitarian movement, spreading harmony and beauty to all, the people most able to benefit were the well-off. As the designs got more rarified, fewer people were able to afford them, and by 1932 the group was no longer in existence.

Josef Hoffman, the principal architect behind the Wiener Werkstätte, was commissioned in 1904 by Adolph Stoclet to design a house in Brussels from scratch. Stoclet was a wealthy industrialist and no expense was spared on the project, which involved contributions from a number of artists, including Klimt. Both Oskar Kokoschka and Egon Schiele, two young artists who were still students, contributed designs, though these were eventually rejected in favour of more established artists.

In 1904 Klimt started on his working designs for an ornamental mosaic, using semi-precious stones as well as enamel to cover three walls. It was to display Klimt's mastery of mosaic, a technique that he had intensely studied on his recent visit to Ravenna. He continued to work on the project for the next five years. The idea behind the frieze was the life cycle – with the tree of life as a central motif. A monumental collaboration between art and architecture, the *Stoclet Frieze* is also perhaps the greatest expression to the Secessionist belief in the importance of the interaction of all the art forms.

*Jurisprudence, 1903. One of the objections Klimt's critics had to this work was that the final painting with its scene of grim torment and misery differed radically from the oil sketch he had submitted.*

The final *Faculty Painting – Jurisprudence –* was exhibited alongside *Philosophy* and *Medicine* in 1903. The painting contains three female figures representing Truth, Justice and Law, who stand over the naked figures of men, including one pinned down by an octopus. The imagery was perceived as shocking in its vengefulness while inappropriately revealing the insecurity of man in the modern world. Klimt was accused in Parliament of 'pornography' and of 'perverted excess'.

With financial help from a patron, Klimt eventually decided to buy *Philosophy* back. *Medicine* and *Jurisprudence* were bought by Koloman Moser his good friend in the Wiener Werkstätte. After Moser's death the works were compulsorily purchased by the Nazis and eventually destroyed by the retreating German army in 1945.

The outcry prompted by the *Faculty Paintings* was like nothing Klimt had faced before. The attack was on many different levels: some questioned the state patronage of the work (the familiar refrain being 'what a waste of money'); others its philosophical content and inherent pessimism; there were also fundamental questions about aesthetics, including whether this should be regarded as art at all. In the face of such bitterness and hostility, the fragility of Klimt's temperament was exposed and the insouciant air he had hitherto adopted was no longer in evidence. In spring 1905 he finally gave way. He withdrew from the commission and shortly afterwards, along with his colleagues Hoffman, Moser and Roller, from the Secession itself.

Philosophy, *1899–1907. The first of the three University ceiling paintings to stir up controversy, with Klimt's detractors baffled by its apparent lack of connection to the realm of Philosophy.*

# CHAPTER 3
# Femmes Fatales

It is clear that Klimt is one of those artists for whom writing or thinking about art is less important than actually doing it. Klimt rarely wrote about art and therefore those wanting to find extra meaning in his life and work have fallen upon the little that is recorded. In an essay entitled 'Commentary on a non-existent self-portrait', he stated, 'I have never painted a self-portrait. I am less interested in myself as a subject for a painting than I am in other people, above all women ... There is nothing special about me. I am a painter who paints day after day from morning to night... Whoever wants to know something about me... ought to look carefully at my pictures.'

One of Klimt's overriding themes is women and, particularly during his Secessionist period, attractive, powerful and seductive women. The concept of the femme fatale – a woman who is dangerous, even fatally so, having the ability to ensnare her lovers and lead them into compromising or deadly situations – is not new and indeed is an archetype of literature and art. In Western culture of the late nineteenth and early twentieth centuries, the femme fatale became a fashionable trope. The women whom Klimt chose to depict in his paintings were often based on allegorical figures from Bible stories and ancient Greek and Roman mythology. The models who posed for these femmes fatales were mostly women known to Klimt and in some cases, women with whom he enjoyed an intimate, sexual relationship. In addition, a couple of the women were the wives of businessmen and leading figures of Viennese society who had commissioned their portraits, and they were also his lovers. During his lifetime Klimt went to great lengths to ensure that these affairs did not reach the ears of his patrons, a scandal of this sort being almost certain to destroy his career.

It is perhaps unsurprising, therefore, that in his portraits of society wives Klimt depicts the strong powerful women whom he was to return to time and again. *Serena Lederer* (1899) and *Gertha Felsovanyi* (1902) are both almost full-length and are attractive, flattering portraits of women married to prosperous Viennese businessman. The tones are muted and their long pale robes softly tumble to the floor. There is, however, something slightly unnerving and ambivalent about their gaze: both stare at the viewer with the same detached air, their haughtiness perhaps suggestive of the fact they are uncomfortable or unwilling to be seen as subordinate.

Serena Lederer, 1899. *In a move clearly designed to flatter and charm, Klimt painted many of his patron's wives including Serena, the wife of industrialist August Lederer. However, in this instance, Serena is thought to have commissioned the portrait herself.*

Nuda Veritas, 1898. Klimt's original illustration that appeared in the Secessionist magazine Ver Sacrum.

Moving Water, 1898. In Klimt's watery world, women are naked and at one with the flowing waves, an erotic image that provoked some criticism.

Klimt was clearly under some constraint himself when creating these portraits of their wives for his patrons. It was in his allegorical Secessionist paintings where he allowed his central theme – the power of women, and the liberating force of sexuality and eroticism – to predominate. In 1899, he produced a second version of *Nuda Veritas*, originally created as an illustration for the Secessionist journal *Ver Sacrum*. In this large painting, a naked red-haired woman holds up the mirror of truth while a serpent lies dead at her feet. In its painted gold frame a quotation by German dramatist Friedrich Schiller in stylized lettering reads, 'If you cannot please everyone with your deeds and your art, please only a few. To please many is bad.' The quotation from Schiller was an attempt to assuage the Viennese public, which would be affronted, Klimt knew, by such a blatant image of a woman, with her pubic hair completely visible. This real life nude was therefore a gauntlet thrown down as a challenge to the idealized beauties of the past. Alongside *Pallas Athene*, his vision of a Greek goddess as self-possessed warrior, *Nuda Veritas* marked the start of a different type of female heroine – one who could bewitch and seduce while operating on instinct and assuming control.

Central to Klimt's idea of the femme fatale was the idea that feminine eroticism could be seen as self-sufficient and impossible to capture. The association with water is key in this respect and with Art Nouveau in general. The symbolist poets and artists of the Romantic era developed the motif of a water nymph or siren, originally found in Greek mythology. The poet Rainer Maria Rilke, composer Claude Debussy and artists Auguste Rodin, Arnold Böcklin and Edward Burne-Jones were amongst those who saw woman as an elementary being tied to nature, who could seduce and destroy in equal measure. In his paintings of femmes fatales, Klimt built on this idea, presenting an underwater world full of shimmering light and dark, in which fish dart, algae and coral grow on rock and women are shown naked, their pale flowing bodies drifting or succumbing to the tide.

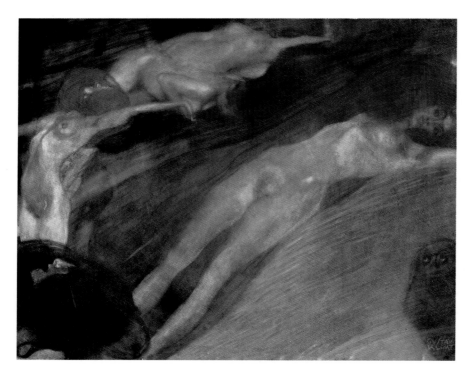

As it was in ancient mythology, water here can be seen as a symbol of the womb and, as such, an emblem of birth, fertility and woman-ness. Consciously or unconsciously, Klimt seems to be making a connection with Sigmund Freud's work about the interpretation of dreams, published in Vienna at the turn of the century. Water here is one of the elements of the unconscious and is associated with intuition and emotion – the supposed realm of the feminine. The ability to see visual echoes between the waves and movement of water and the curves of the female form helped Klimt and others to define the linear, flowing curves of the Art Nouveau graphic style.

Mermaids, *1899. A curious painting in which Klimt appears to be symbolically linking women and water again, although this time the women are disembodied with their heads wrapped in dark shrouds.*

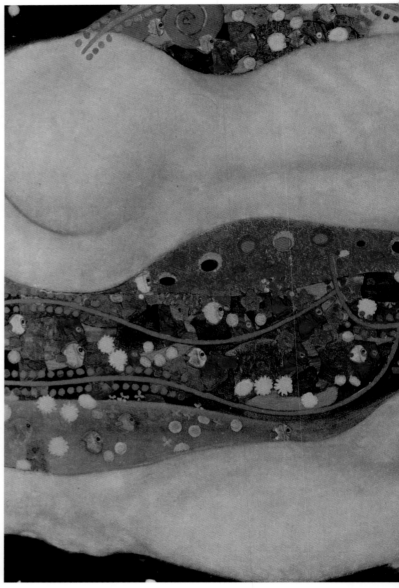

Left: Water Serpents I, *1904–07. Klimt's painting of two women locked together in a lover's embrace, is made more respectable by its seductive gold patterning and exquisite details.*

In these watery visions, women swim as fish and the associations of eroticism and sensuality come into play as their naked bodies float or languidly glide in the water. In *Moving Water* (1898), sensuous, naked female bodies stretch out luxuriously, abandoning themselves to the waves. Stranger still is *Water Nymphs (Silverfish)* (c.1899) in which

the faces of two women with fixed, almost diabolical expressions, appear in the gloom wrapped in a dappled shroud – a cocoon that curiously seems almost sperm-like. In both *Water Serpents I* (1904–07) and *Water Serpents II* (1904–07), Klimt presents a world of women in which men are totally absent. The women themselves seem to take pleasure in their own eroticism. In *Water Serpents I*, a woman merges almost completely into a fish, her hands covering her bare torso, eyes shut and mouth open in ecstasy. In *Water Serpents II*, four female figures swim together as one in a tightly packed shoal, with their hair entangled by hundreds of tiny plants, their enmeshed bodies suggestive of both metamorphosis and an unknowable, inaccessible sexual intimacy.

Water Serpents II, *1904–07. The sheer beauty of these women with their pale sinuous bodies and plant-entangled hair again helped to make this painting more palatable to Viennese society.*

Right: Judith I, 1901. *In the first of his interpretations of the biblical story of Judith and Holofernes, Klimt's main focus is in creating a strong and powerful heroine – one of his femmes fatales.*

Far right: Judith II (Salome), 1909. *In the second version of the Judith and Holofernes story painted some eight years later, Judith is less idealized, her hands are like claws and her face and posture more menacing.*

*Judith and the Head of Holofernes*, also known as *Judith I* (1901), marks the start of Klimt's golden style and is another of his celebrated femmes fatales. Gold leaf abounds in this painting – the difference between this and earlier works is that the gold becomes the dominant material and is incorporated fully into the structure of the painting. The ornamentation of the painting is lavish and is mirrored in the frame, showing the Byzantine influence picked up by Klimt on his trip to Ravenna in Italy.

In Klimt's interpretation of the Old Testament story, Judith stares challengingly, even triumphantly out at the viewer. She holds the decapitated head of Holofernes, Nebuchadnezzar's general, who was waging war on the town. It is a symbolic image overlaid by the association between sexuality and death, with Judith's head tilted backwards, her eyes half closed and her mouth open, seemingly enjoying a moment of ecstasy. In no sense does Judith resemble the stereotypical portrayal of a biblical heroine

*Mosaics of Emperor Justinianus (left) and Empress Theodora (right) in the Basilica of San Vitale in Ravenna.*

who has executed such a grim deed. With her heavily lidded eyes, cloud of dark hair, unabashed stare and sumptuous gold collar, she looks as if she would be more at home singing in one of Vienna's fashionable nightclubs. Klimt's Judith therefore scandalized those who set eyes on her: some believed that Klimt had mistaken Judith for Salome and tried to re-appropriate the painting whenever it appeared.

Critics have described how they see Klimt's Judith as a mistress of her own desire and as a representation of both the yearning and fear that was prevalent in the male erotic imagination of the time. Interestingly, in his 1909 version of Judith, Klimt makes some changes that would seem to put a different slant on his intentions second time around. In *Judith II*, the gold and decorative elements are reduced. Judith's body is turned slightly, her hands are twisted above Holofernes' disembodied head and her expression is impassive, if a little more tense. Overall, the charming insouciance of the first portrait has disappeared, to be replaced by a woman who looks indeed like she might have committed a terrible act. The two paintings of Judith seem to sum up Klimt's contradictory and ambivalent feelings towards his femmes fatales and, seemingly, to women in general. On the one hand they completely fascinated him and made him desire them; at the same time, they made him extremely fearful.

The dark-haired, imposing model Klimt used for both his portraits of Judith was Adele Bloch-Bauer, who is believed also to have been his mistress. Bloch-Bauer was the wife of one of his patrons, the sugar magnate and banker Ferdinand Bloch-Bauer, so Klimt was clearly taking a great risk in becoming sexually involved with her. Klimt had numerous affairs, mostly with his models, and was the father to 14 illegitimate children. He avoided scandal and managed to keep these relationships out of the public eye during his lifetime, but several of his models won court cases to establish the legal rights of their offspring once he died.

Despite his unprepossessing appearance – he was a stocky, hirsute

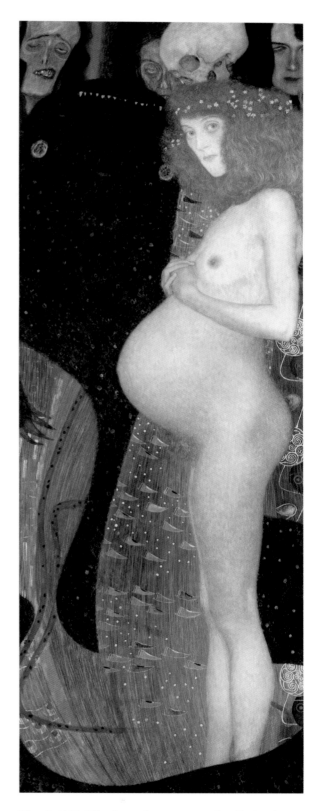

Hope I, 1903. *Klimt knew this painting might offend and it was first exhibited three years after it was finished. A special frame was built with closing doors to hide the protruding belly.*

Hope II, 1907–08. Klimt treats his
second Hope painting as an allegory.
The expectant woman is covered up
with richly decorated robes, her head is
bowed and a group of women worship
at her feet.

man with a square jaw – Klimt famously loved women and undoubtedly relied on his position as a successful artist to win over the beautiful young models who came to his studio to sit for him. While these women clearly loved the fact that Klimt could make them look so glamorous, there is no evidence that he exploited or abused the women in any way. An unrepentant but ardent suitor, he seems to have chosen affairs with his models over marriage as a way of establishing the central importance of art in his life. Relationships with women, except possibly for his intense association with Emilie Flöge, came second. This meant that he enjoyed the best of both worlds – a ready supply of beautiful women to admire, seduce and paint while remaining free of the complications or daily drudgery that he feared would drag him away from his art.

Marie Zimmerman (known as Mizzi) was another of his regular models and Klimt was the father of two of her sons. She has been identified in his earlier Impressionistic work *Schubert at the Piano* (1899), where she stands to the right of the composer, illuminated by candlelight and pregnant with Klimt's child. She posed again for *Hope I* (1903) although in this instance Klimt altered details of her facial features while leaving her flame red hair true to life. This painting, with Mizzi's unabashed stare, pale naked body and pregnant belly highly visible, was considered highly offensive to Klimt's contemporaries. As with so many depictions of the female and the feminine, Klimt's work is ambiguous. On the one hand, it can be read as a lyrical and joyous celebration of womanhood and new life; on the other, there are various masks, skulls and monsters surrounding the pregnant woman, which are also suggestive of disease and death. Declared obscene when it was exhibited in 1903, *Hope I* was bought by Fritz Waerndorfer, one of Klimt's patrons, who kept it enclosed within a special cabinet at his home.

*The Three Ages of Woman, 1905. The three figures in this work represent childhood, maturity and old age and exemplify one of Klimt's mature themes: the life cycle. Awarded the gold medal at the International Exhibition of Art in Rome in 1911.*

*Hope II* (1907/08), painted several years later, features a different model and an altogether less ambivalent tone. In the second version, the destructive symbolic elements have withered away and the woman's body is covered up to her bare breasts in a beautifully ornamental sheath-like rich gold robe. At her feet, three women with their eyes closed appear to be praying, relating back to Klimt's allegorical theme of the Madonna and Child.

Klimt's obsession with the feminine and the transience of beauty resurfaces again in the *Three Ages of Woman* (1905). In his allegorical treatment of the life cycle – childhood, maturity and old age – an older woman stands to the left of the painting, with one bony hand by her side and the other holding her long locks in front of her face. Emphasizing the inescapable passage of time, the raw, naturalistic treatment of her flesh seems almost contemporary, as if Klimt had studied Lucien Freud's fleshy nudes. The other two figures – a mother and child – rest on each other's bodies, their studied poses, pink cheeks and rosebud mouths being more typical of Klimt's idealized beauties. Again, striking another contemporary note, the whole painting is divided into different sections, including two black squares, and grey and brown panels with a rain of tiny white specks like tumbling stars. In addition, the figures stand within their own decorative space, richly littered with gold and veils of gauzy material. Here Klimt uses space in a dynamic and challenging way, causing our eye to dart around the work as the movement between the figures and the ground constantly shifts.

While creating some of his most celebrated allegorical works, Klimt was also busily fulfilling commissions for his patrons, including in 1905 *Portrait of Margarethe Stonborough-Wittgenstein* and a year later *Portrait of Fritza Riedler*. The first of these was a portrait of the daughter of Karl Wittgenstein, one of his most significant patrons, on the eve of her marriage to an American doctor, Thomas Stonborough. As with previous society portraits, Margarethe is tall, imposing, dressed in a long white frock and appears somewhat detached from her surroundings. Behind her head there are various panels, including a central gold embellished panel, a nod to his richly allegorical paintings. It seems that Klimt is more interested in the composition as a whole rather than the sitter, a point borne out by the fact that Margarethe herself disliked the work and removed it from her wall as soon as she could.

Margarethe Stonborough-Wittgenstein, 1905. *This portrait of one of his patron's daughters was painted on the occasion of Margarethe's marriage to an American doctor.*

*Portrait of Fritza Riedler* takes this sense of cross-pollination between the commissioned portraits and the allegorical paintings a whole stage further. The German-born Fritza Riedler was the wife of a professor of engineering at the University of Vienna and the couple moved in the circles of Viennese high society. Between 1904 and 1905 Riedler visited Klimt's studio, where he made numerous studies of her before embarking on this daring portrait. In it, Klimt takes a series of imaginative risks, creating tension between the abstract and the figurative parts of the painting. The armchair in which she sits has become a two-dimensional outline filled in with gold and silver eye or mouth-shaped motifs. The gold and silver are picked up by the small squares dotted across the background wall. On the carpet beneath her feet, there are a couple of squares that resemble eyes or mouths – motifs that are generally seen as symbols of eroticism.

Riedler's grey dress is insubstantial, almost a washy sketch, and gets swallowed up by the patterning on the armchair. As in the portrait of Margarethe Stonborough-Wittgenstein, Klimt has placed a simplified shape behind Riedler's head, in this case a rough semi-circle. The device serves to frame and draw attention to her face while at the same time recalling ancient decorative Egyptian art and, more particularly, the headdresses used by Diego Velázquez (1599–1660) in his portraits of the Spanish Infanta.

We stare up at Riedler or she looks down on us, depending on the way you look at it. She has, as with so many of Klimt's portraits of women, great poise, but there is also a melancholic air about her that creates a sense of realism in the midst of such an abstract and stylized portrayal. The use of gold and silver leaf in the delicate small rectangles distributed over the surface and the two golden bars to the left show the growing importance that he attached to the decorative qualities of his work as well as their integration into the overall design. This is a development that was to find its full expression a year later in Klimt's magnificent portrait of Adele Bloch-Bauer.

The portrait of Riedler marks the beginning of Klimt's celebrated 'golden phase', generally agreed to be between 1906 and 1908. Within these years, Klimt was a master at the height of his powers, producing gilded depictions of fin-de-siècle women, which manage to be abstract and representational, conservative and modern.

The wife of Ferdinand Bloch-Bauer, an Austrian Jewish banker 17 years her senior, Adele Bloch-Bauer was the model for both of Klimt's portraits of Judith, and some also believe that she was his lover. Undeniably Adele was a beautiful, elegant woman whom Klimt adored and their relationship (whether consummated or not) started in the 1890s. The Bloch-Bauers were connoisseurs of art and part of the Viennese cultural set; Adele ran a salon from their home which attracted leading composers, artists and writers.

*Fritza Riedler, 1906. Klimt's portrait of another wealthy Viennese woman clearly shows the transition of his work away from realism towards a more stylized approach favouring decoration and pattern. It also shows the influence of Velázquez' Portrait of the Infanta Maria Teresa of Spain.*

# THE KISS

Along with the *Mona Lisa*, Gustav Klimt's *The Kiss* is one of the most reproduced images in the world. Few people have probably seen the real thing, housed in the Galerie Belvedere museum in the Belvedere Palace, Vienna. Yet countless copies of the work (on everything from posters and greeting cards to mugs and key rings) have made this work one of the most popular and inescapable images of our time.

What gives *The Kiss* its enduring appeal? Painted by Gustav Klimt between 1907 and 1908, at the height of what has become known as his Golden Period, the work is oil on canvas with added silver and gold leaf. A large square painting, it measures 180 × 180cm (71 × 71 inches), and its focus is the two life-size figures – a man and a woman – locked in a sensuous embrace. The lovers are shown kneeling on a carpet of tiny flowers, their bodies entwined by a sinuous outline around their flowing, highly decorated, rich gold robes.

Although he clearly intended the painting to be seen as an allegory, as was also true of many similar paintings drawing upon biblical stories and myths, Klimt was not explicit about his intentions. This has led some to believe that the couple depicted in the work could represent Adam and Eve – Adam with his crown of vines and Eve with her crown of flowers. Others have seen this as a representation of the Ovid narrative, the moment when Apollo kisses Daphne.

Perhaps what is most interesting about this painting are the many and various different interpretations that viewers and critics alike have brought to it. Many see this work as the quintessential expression of one of the deepest passions known to mankind, sensual love. To other observers this depiction of a loving affair between a man and woman is a new development in Klimt's oeuvre, given that many of the male and female relationships he had previously depicted appear much less harmonious. Closer inspection of *The Kiss* reveals that the lovers are not actually kissing, which seems to reflect the fact that people see want they want to see rather than what is actually there. Klimt clearly saw the painting as an allegorical work, and it is this ability to lend an ordinary romantic or even erotic encounter higher spiritual meaning that gives it such charm.

Aside from the passionate subject matter, what distinguishes *The Kiss* is Klimt's unique approach, seen here in all its glory: the curving lines, alluring use of gold and brilliant jewel-like ornamentation. Drawing on elements from Byzantine mosaics, which Klimt had seen at Ravenna in Italy, and from the bold patterning of the English Arts and Craft movement, this is Klimt at the height of his powers. Produced around the turn of the century, when Vienna was going though its own golden period, this painting is one of the most celebrated examples of the Viennese Art Nouveau (or Jugendstil).

Klimt was one of the greatest exponents of Art Nouveau, an ornamental style of art characterized by its use of a sinuous, flowing line and organic forms, but he did not invent it. As a movement, Art Nouveau flourished throughout Europe and the United States between about 1890 and 1910. Its curvy lines and the floral and plant-inspired motifs were employed in many art forms, including painting, architecture, interior design, posters, jewellery and glass design.

Unlike the Faculty Paintings, made for the ceiling of the University of Vienna's Great Hall and deemed pornographic, *The Kiss* was well received when it was first publicly exhibited in 1908. It was bought unfinished by the Austrian government and has resided in the Belvedere Museum ever since. The museum paid 25,000 crowns (about $240,000 today) and if it were ever sold, it would probably reach one of the highest sums ever paid for a painting in the world. By way of comparison, when Klimt's portrait of Adele Bloch-Bauer came up for sale in 2006, it reached a staggering $135 million.

The Kiss, 1907–08. *Over the course of his career, Klimt made several paintings of two figures locked in a passionate embrace. Unarguably the most famous one, it is often held up as his greatest work.*

Commissioned by Ferdinand in 1903, Adele's portrait took Klimt nearly four years to complete (and was followed up with a second portrait that he finished in 1912). Painted at the height of his golden period, the naturalistic elements – Adele's thin pale face and hands – are surrounded by rich gold decoration and a swirling mass of ovals, blocks and spirals, drawing upon a range of Byzantine and Egyptian motifs. The sitter – if indeed she is seated; her vaporous body has been dematerialized – hovers in a sea of gold. This excess of gold, the swirling spirals and the multitude of Egyptian eyes lends the portrait connotations of magic and transformation as well as an allure and an exoticism. Klimt has created the perfect balance between the realistic and the abstract elements in this painting. Adele's face, with its sad eyes and slightly mournful expression, is compelling and draws the viewer in, while the flurry of ornamental motifs and sumptuous gold creates an altogether more visionary work.

The use of a choker around Adele's neck has intrigued critics and commentators. The device, which has the effect of separating her head from her body and from the decorative elements, is not new to Klimt: there are chokers in the form of scarves and neckpieces in other portraits, including *Judith I* (Adele again), *Fritza Riedler* and *Emilie Flöge*. Some critics feel that this fractured view of the female body was Klimt's subconscious way of being able to exert control over women. Other psychological interpretations have also concentrated on a more morbid aspect to the portrait, seeing the disembodied head and shoulders of Adele Bloch-Bauer as imprisoned and locked inside a gold metal casing.

As already noted, *The Kiss* (1907) is one of Klimt's greatest and most celebrated works. It did not come from nowhere, for similar figures – a man and a woman locked in a close embrace – exist in his mural work for the *Beethoven Frieze* and the *Stoclet Frieze*. In relation to his femmes fatales, *The Kiss* would seem initially to offer a much more traditional view of woman as yielding to the more dominant male. However, critics have brought a range of opinions and interpretations to the work, which offer, at the very least, some alternative readings of this straightforward narrative.

While hardly the dominant figure (unlike the many dominant female figures in earlier paintings), the woman appears to have more control over the situation than the rather more sexually assertive man. Her face remains impassive and even slightly unyielding – could this indicate some sort of reluctance on her part? Are her tense hands and feet a further indication of this?

The ornamentation on the lovers' clothing in *The Kiss* is also strongly contrasted. The woman's robe is adorned with colourful circles whereas the man's is based on black and white squares. Using emblems to differentiate between male and female is not new; throughout the history of art there are examples of artists using symbolism to signify difference. Men and male attributes are often equated with geometric or angular forms and women with circular motifs, such as the moon. Some have speculated that in this juxtaposition in *The Kiss*, as well as in the woman's self-absorption, Klimt saw some kind of innate disjuncture between the sexes which made fulfillment an impossibility. This theory seems to gain some credibility when you examine the evidence of his own experience, in particular with Emilie Flöge, who may have been the model used here and with whom it is believed he never enjoyed a loving relationship. There is a danger here, of course, that reading personal or biographical meaning into the work reduces it. Ultimately, *The Kiss* remains outside such readings, offering us a powerful symbolic declaration of erotic love that achieves its effect by drawing upon a wealth of gold and rich ornamental detail.

Also in 1907, Klimt painted *Danaë*. The painting is based on the classical myth in which the god Zeus rescues Danaë from her father. He, believing her offspring will kill him, has locked her away in a chamber. Zeus impregnates Danaë in a golden shower and in Klimt's unabashedly erotic painting a torrent of gold pieces are shown cascading between her huge thighs. An explicit image, Danaë's pale naked body is shown curled up in a cocoon of gauzy, contrasting black material. Her soporific expression, parted lips and long red dishevelled hair suggest a woman who is not at the point of orgasm but whose self-absorption is complete. Despite its decorative elements, and the fig leaf of respectability that it gains from being based on a classical myth, Danaë's frank eroticism is something that Klimt would return to in his later portrayals of women, in particular the erotic drawings of lovers and of reclining nudes that he made and exhibited from 1910 onwards.

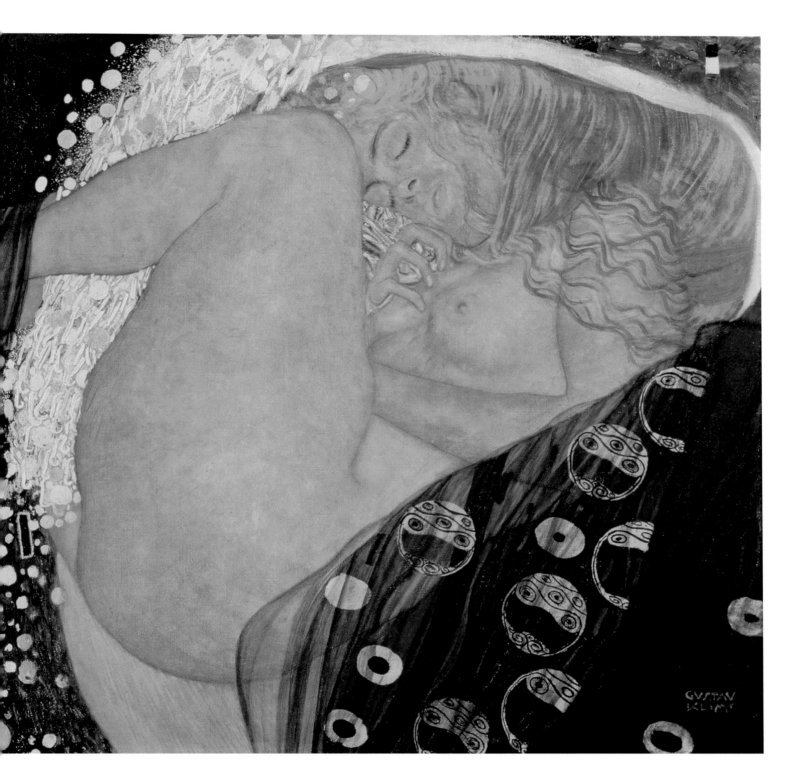

Danaë, 1907. *Based on the myth of Zeus, who visits Danaë when imprisoned by her father the King of Argos, this painting has an erotic charge that supersedes its allegorical significance.*

# CHAPTER 4
# Landscapes

Around the time that Klimt was creating his golden allegorical paintings, a new generation of artists was starting to make its presence felt in Vienna. Chief among these young artists were Egon Schiele (1890–1918) and Oskar Kokoschka (1886–1980), both of whom revered the older artist and his work. Unlike Klimt, neither of these artists bore the heavy mantle of the classical past on their shoulders. Both were versatile painters who excelled at drawing and who painted figurative subjects, including portraits and landscapes.

Egon Schiele was the son of a stationmaster in the small town of Tulln, Lower Austria. Isolated and reserved at home and school, where he found learning difficult, he spent much of his childhood obsessively drawing trains. In 1906 he applied to study at the Kunstgewerbeschule, the institution where Klimt had studied, and was accepted. Within a year, Schiele was being mentored by Klimt, who was noted for being generous to younger artists and who clearly recognized in Schiele a raw talent as well as similar preoccupations when it came to subject matter.

*Self-portrait, Egon Schiele, 1906. A charcoal self-portrait of Egon Schiele, aged 16. Schiele idolized Klimt as a student and the two first met in 1908.*

Although Klimt and his closest associates Hoffman, Moser and Roller had broken with the Secession in 1905, the group continued to exhibit together and in 1908 held what was to be their final exhibition. While Klimt showed 16 works, the focus of the exhibition in 1908 was on the invited artists – including Schiele and Kokoschka – and a range of international artists, including Munch, Bonnard, Matisse, Gauguin and Van Gogh. This meant that Klimt came up close against the dramatic, boldly coloured and highly charged landscapes of both the Fauves and the Expressionists. The experience was decisive for Klimt. Not only did it precipitate his rupture with the Secessionist group altogether, but it also made him feel that his golden style was outdated and inferior to the work of these other artists. Once Klimt decided to break away from what became known as the Klimt Group, he felt isolated and no longer sure of the support of the young artists who had up to this point adored him. He confided to a friend that, 'The young no longer understand me. They go elsewhere. I don't even know whether they appreciate my work any more. It's a bit early for that to happen to me, but it happens to every artist. The young will always want to take everything that's already there by storm and pull it down. I shan't get angry with them over it.'

*Church in Unterach on the Attersee, 1916. Standing on the other side of the lake, Klimt used binoculars to capture this view of the church and village of Unterach.*

If Klimt was rattled by the sense that his work might appear overly ornate and decorative when compared with some of his European counterparts, he continued to pursue an entirely separate body of work – his landscapes. Out of a total of 230 paintings, Klimt produced 54 landscapes. He first began to focus on landscape as a subject matter in its own right in 1897, when he was invited by Emilie Flöge's family to spend his summer holidays on Lake Attersee, a picturesque rural area in Upper Austria. The landscapes reflect the summer weather he enjoyed in the tranquil environs of Attersee: he is not known to have painted any winter landscapes.

Klimt first exhibited landscapes in 1898 at the inaugural exhibition of the Viennese Secession. Over the next decade these were to prove popular and sold well, and today are a much admired and celebrated part of his oeuvre. By and large these landscapes are unadorned – there's almost no gold – they feature no people and they are not designed to tell any specific story. Quite simply, Klimt enjoyed painting the landscapes around the lake, as he found it very relaxing and a change from the pressured life he was leading in Vienna. If he made sketches or preparatory drawings, none of them has survived. He worked *en plein air* – painting directly in the landscape – as the Impressionists did. Sometimes he would set up an easel by the shores of the lake, at other times he would go out in a small boat to paint. He also made use of aids such as a cut-out view finder, binoculars or even a telescope to home in on a particular view. Usually, he finished these paintings back in his Viennese studio.

*Morning by the Pond, 1899. With its hazy morning light and shimmering reflections, this early landscape recalls the atmospheric work of Impressionist Claude Monet.*

In complete opposition to his allegorical paintings, Klimt's landscapes are devoid of any human presence. Mostly they show us inaccessible places: buildings that are almost completely covered in vegetation or whole expanses of water or fields trapped under a low horizon. As some critics have remarked, it is like looking through a spyhole when suddenly the details come sharply into focus, allowing you to experience a moment that is almost spiritual in its quiet contemplation.

Though Klimt's landscapes do not typically focus on any kind of living being, an early landscape, *After the Rain* (1898–99) does feature animals. The canvas is elongated, which focuses our attention on the chickens wandering randomly in a field beneath trees. It is almost as if we are looking through a narrow doorway onto the scene. The chickens are painted loosely, but their main purpose appears to be to add colour and shape to the overall pattern of this softly painted and serene landscape.

While aware of the artists who were creating Impressionist and Post-Impressionist landscapes, Klimt was less interested in the changing effects of light or weather. His landscapes are at once stylized and detailed – a cross between abstraction and representation. Klimt mostly chose the square format for his landscapes. As he revealed, 'This format makes it possible to bathe the subject in an atmosphere of peace. Through the square the picture becomes part of a universal whole.' Within his squares, a field of tiny marks appears to represent every leaf, tree or stem and the effect is that the overall, undifferentiated plane becomes the subject of the work. In this respect Klimt's landscapes – like his figure paintings – are symbolic, revealing his aim of aspiring to some sort of universal harmony.

Within his square format, Klimt was adventurous in compositional terms with his landscape work. It seems that the uniformity of this repeated format allowed him to experiment. So, for example, he would make the horizon level lower or higher, or crop the view so that trees or other elements would sit to the side or outside of his frame. It is this cropping aspect to his landscape work – the hint at what was going on outside or around the canvas – that makes them seem so modern.

Spending summers on Lake Attersee gave Klimt the opportunity to develop various ways of painting water. *Calm Pond in the Park of Schloss Kammer* (1899) is a beautiful image in which Klimt eschews all detail to allow us to focus solely on the slabs of land and water. The off-centre composition with its left-sided, dark overhanging trees is offset by the subtleties of the surface of the pale water. In its stillness and sense of lyricism, the image recalls the landscapes

*After the Rain, 1899. Another early landscape that has a distinctly Impressionist feel with its gentle light and soft daubs of paint.*

of Claude Monet. *Island on the Attersee* (1901) is an early minimal landscape with a modern feel in which the low horizon focuses our attention on the calm expanse of turquoise water. Composed from short, flecked brushstrokes, the water fills up nearly the entire surface, almost engulfing the distant island, an indeterminate dark brooding shape to the top right of the canvas. Compare this to the later work *Church in Unterach on the Attersee* (1916), a dynamic diagonal composition in which the layers of brightly coloured buildings and foliage are reflected in the shimmering lake, striking an altogether more light-filled, positive and harmonious note.

Beechwood Forest, *1903. Klimt made several forest scenes and they all follow the same pattern: row upon row of trees standing on a bed of leaves.*

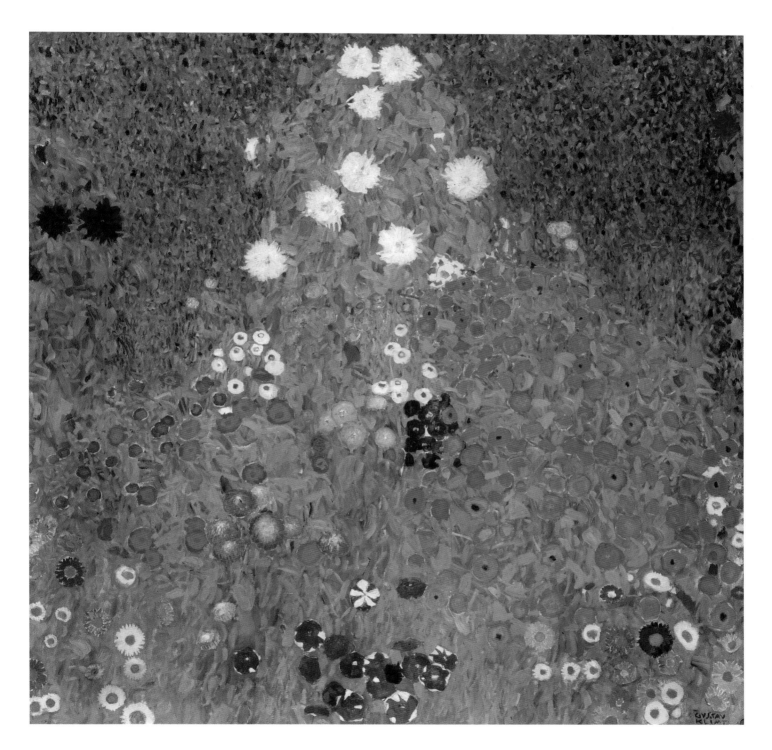

His forest scenes follow a similar pattern. Trees were a recurring motif and in the early 1900s he painted several relatively similar scenes of a network of bare tree trunks upright on a carpet of leaves. Klimt was drawn to these 'empty' forests and walked through the woods at 6.00 a.m. each day while on his summer vacation around Lake Attersee. He noted the fine distinctions between the different trees – fir, pine, birch and beech, for example – and carefully recorded these in his paintings of woods. While relying on

Flower Garden, *1905–07. The fact that Klimt adopted a square format for most of his landscapes allowed him to fill every inch of the canvas, in this case with a field of grass and garden flowers.*

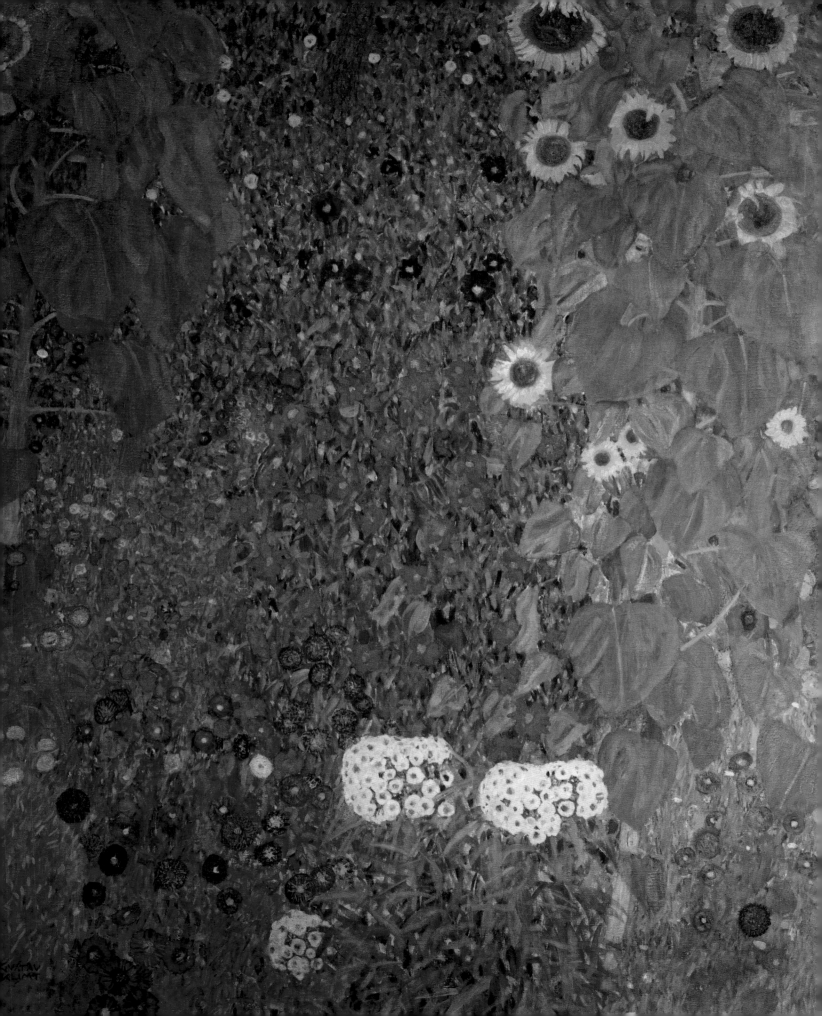

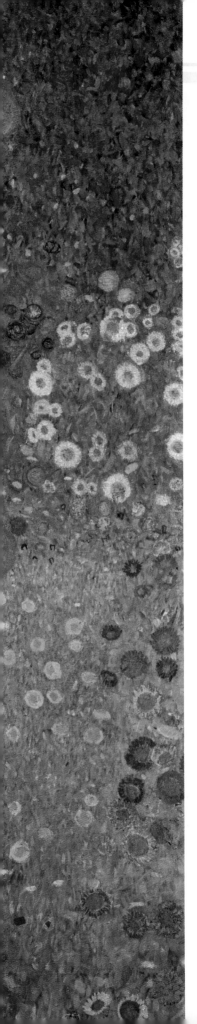

repetition and a sense of pattern, these poetic landscapes also communicate a particularly strong atmosphere of melancholy. In *Beechwood Forest* (1903), row upon row of silver beech trees are depicted on a carpet of orange leaves: there are no figures or creatures, nothing to interrupt the visual rhythm of the whole painting – it is a silent and meditative world.

Many of Klimt's calm landscapes recall Japanese art. Klimt built up his own collection of Oriental art, including Japanese woodblock prints, some Chinese paintings, and other objects including Noh masks, kimonos and porcelain. He sometimes adopted the narrow vertical format from Japanese prints in his work. His use of an overlapping technique to suggest distance, placing some objects in the foreground to partially cover other more distant objects, also came from Japanese painting. The way he played with the level of the horizon to balance it against other elements is another technique he learnt from studying Oriental art.

Clearly Klimt's landscapes provided him with a literal retreat from his world in Vienna, where he had obligations to his patrons as well as to all the other artists with whom he associated. He was also freed up by being able to paint directly from nature and to dispense with the more ostentatious aspects of his better-known golden and ornamental paintings. Klimt loved nature and the natural world and his own garden filled with trees and shrubs was a great source of inspiration for him and also helped to stabilize his mood when he was less than satisfied with his work. *Farm Garden (Flower Garden)* (1905–06) is a square painting filled with flowers and shrubs from his own garden – every inch of the canvas being packed with leaves, stems and blooms. The density of the foliage creates an overall pattern that resembles a piece of fabric. This work, along with a similar painting *Farm Garden with Sunflowers* (1905–06), is faintly reminiscent of Monet's waterlily paintings in the sense that they appear to extend beyond the canvas in a desire to show us the infinite nature of the universe.

Farm Garden with Sunflowers, 1907. *Although Klimt has featured sunflowers here, they do not predominate over the rest of the flowers in the garden – his interest appears to be in the effect of the whole rather than the parts.*

Rose Bushes Under the Trees, *1905. Klimt's approach here –*
*building up the dense layers of vegetation using small daubs*
*of paint – recalls the Impressionists' pointillist technique.*

*Rosesbushes Under the Trees* and *Orchard* (both c. 1905) and *Poppy Field* (1907) extend the idea of repeated pattern even further. Each dizzying landscape is built up using hundreds of tiny dots or slabs of colour, giving the overall effect of a mosaic or even the view offered through a kaleidoscope. *Sunflower* (1907), a giant sunflower appearing out of a mosaic-like flowerbed, is thought to have inspired the composition for *The Kiss*. Emilie Flöge posed for photographs in front of these sunflowers and this resulted in Klimt's celebrated painting a year later.

Poppy Field, 1907. *There is a real sense of perspective in this landscape, as the distant hedges and high horizon accentuate the immensity of the poppy field.*

Sunflower, 1907. *Klimt painted sunflowers on several occasions. It is quite likely that he saw Van Gogh's paintings of sunflowers as the Dutch post-impressionist artist showed at the Secession exhibition of 1903.*

Schloss Kammer (an eighteenth-century villa on Lake Attersee) was another subject that Klimt returned to in his landscapes several times. *Schloss Kammer on Lake Attersee I* (1908) is a composition in mainly sludgy browns and olive greens. The villa nestles amongst foliage and the painting's main focus is the muddy reflections in the water. Klimt made two other versions of this scene over the next couple of years, and in the second one the colour has switched to a brighter green with the emphasis on the surrounding vegetation, rather than the water. The third one is altogether more stylized – Klimt painted it from a boat on the lake for his friend and model Adele Bloch-Bauer and the flowers and touches of red give it a jauntier note.

Schloss Kammer on Lake Attersee I, *1908. Klimt painted several versions of Schloss Kammer, an eighteenth-century villa rising above the lake.*

The Park, *1910.*
*With more than*
*two-thirds of the*
*painting occupied*
*by the trees'*
*foliage, Klimt*
*strives to record*
*every single leaf.*
*At the same time,*
*the overall sense*
*of the work is*
*of a tapestry or*
*mosaic.*

Klimt was aware of the new technique of Pointillism developed by the French Impressionist artists Georges Seurat and Paul Signac; the latter had exhibited at the Secession exhibition of 1900 in Vienna. Klimt adapted this technique for his own purposes. He made use of small, distinct dots of colour applied in patterns to form an image but, unlike the Pointillists, he never expressed an interest in utilizing optics in his work or creating illusions of depth. *The Park* (1910) is almost all foliage, apart from some dark vertical lines depicting trunks at the bottom. The great mass of blue, green and yellow dots form a decorative whole, denying the painting any real depth but at the same time creating a real sense of atmosphere and lyricism. Only after a little while do patterns emerge and shift before your eyes, revealing the real impact of the work. One of his most celebrated landscapes, *The Park* initially started life outside but ended up being finished in Klimt's studio.

Farm House in Upper Austria, *1911–12. There is a definite shift in this painting towards a looser, more Impressionistic style. The texture of the wooden hut and the greyish purple tones suggest the influence of Van Gogh.*

Other later Klimt landscapes also borrow elements from Post Impressionism – whether the pointillist technique, the undulating brushwork or the muted green, yellow and blue palette. In *Farmhouse in Upper Austria* (1911–12) the brushstrokes appear looser and less tightly packed and the deserted wooden building itself with its grainy mauve planks looks almost like something Van Gogh could have painted. In *Avenue in the Park of Schloss Kammer*, another work from the same year, Klimt depicts an avenue of gnarled trees. The fact that pattern seems less important here than the expressive nature of the work, suggests Klimt is taking a more modern approach akin to that of both Van Gogh and Cézanne. Perhaps the most significant thing about some of Klimt's most mature landscapes is the heightened level of emotional engagement. Not only do they reflect the artist's love of nature, they increase our own understanding and appreciation of the natural world by evoking a range of moods from tranquillity to despair.

Avenue in the Park of Schloss Kammer, *1912. One of Klimt's most expressive landscapes in which the view through the avenue of gnarled trees is reminiscent of both Van Gogh and Cézanne.*

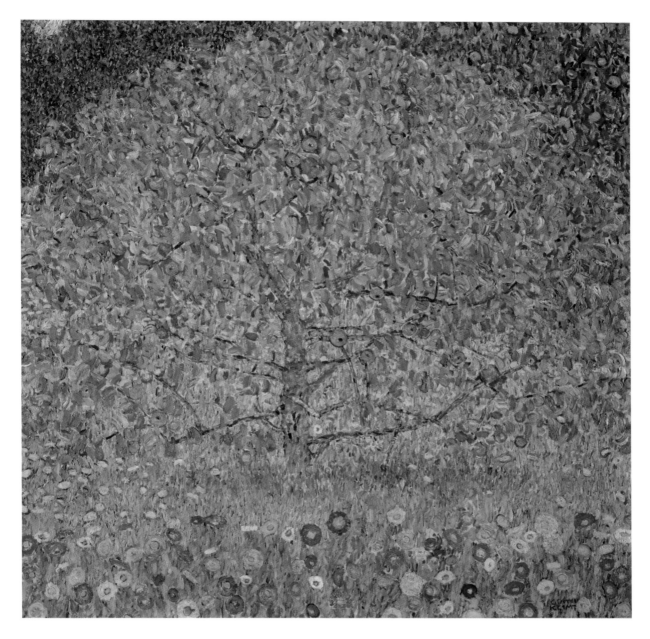

Apple Tree I, *1912. This brightly coloured work with its blooming flowers in the foreground and red apples punctuating the trees appears to be a joyous comment on nature's abundance.*

A darker restless, mood is expressed in *Apple Tree II*, a landscape from 1916. Klimt painted at least three pictures of apple trees, and *Apple Tree II* differs from the all-over patterning and harmonious approach that Klimt adopted for *Apple Tree I* (1912). In both versions Klimt did not attempt to paint the whole tree, but rather presents an off-centre view in which the branches extend to the side and top of the image. In *Apple Tree II* the background is sketchy; the ground a series of hastily applied green brushstrokes with a series of blue and green marks indicating further trees in the distance. The apple tree itself is unrealistic; Klimt depicts the apples as solid dots of colour with a thick outline and this non-naturalistic treatment recalls the work of his younger colleague Egon Schiele.

*Apple Tree II, 1916. Klimt's second painting of an apple tree with its scudding clouds and darker sky evokes a far less harmonious mood. In 1916 Klimt was well aware of the horrific events unfolding across Europe.*

Klimt's landscapes were well regarded by his contemporaries and were bought by a range of patrons. Industrialist Karl Wittgenstein bought three, including the allegorical *Life is a Struggle (The Golden Knight)* (1903), a gold embellished painting of a knight on a horse in front of a mosaic of flowers. He also bought *Sunflower*, perhaps seeing in both some reflection of his struggle to make it to the top of his own profession. Aside from their painting of Lake Attersee, Ferdinand and Adele Bloch-Bauer acquired *Birch Forest* (1903) and *Apple Tree I* (1912), while the Lederers also acquired several landscapes, some of which were later destroyed by fire. The most significant patron of Klimt as a landscape painter was the industrialist Viktor Zuckerkandl, whose collection included *Rosebushes Under the Trees* (c.1905), *Poppy Field* (1907) and *Apple Tree II* (1916).

Life is a Struggle (The Golden Knight), 1903. *This is a rare instance of an animal appearing in Klimt's work. A golden knight also appears in the* Beethoven Frieze *– psychologically it seems interesting that Klimt was drawn to the motif of a knight in shining armour.*

# CHAPTER 5
# The Later Works

If Klimt's golden phase came to glorious fruition with his 1907 *Portrait of Adele Bloch-Bauer I*, it also marked the beginning of some noticeably different traits in his artistic direction. In 1909, at the breakaway group's second and final exhibition in Vienna, Klimt saw at first hand the work of European artists, including Edvard Munch, Paul Gauguin, Vincent Van Gogh, Henri Matisse and Pierre Bonnard. Klimt was inspired but also a little overwhelmed as their expressive work made him realize his own work by contrast was rigid, stylized and lacked the ability to communicate psychological truths. Later that year, Klimt travelled to Paris, where he not only saw a good deal more of the Fauves' intensely coloured paintings but also discovered the work of Henri de Toulouse-Lautrec. This, combined with the raw emotion that he recognized in younger artists like Schiele and Kokoschka, gave Klimt the impetus to make some important stylistic changes. From 1910 he developed a new freer style that dispensed with the gold and the more excessive decorative elements.

In 1910, Klimt was given an individual exhibition at the 9th Biennale in Venice. His room was designed by the Wiener Werkstätte and was very well received. The city bought *Judith II* – the painting still hangs in the Palazzo di Ca' Pesaro on the Grand Canal. The National Gallery of Modern Art in Rome also acquired *The Three Ages of Woman*. Some Italian critics, however, including some of the Futurist artists, saw Klimt's work as decadent and excessive.

A year later, *Death and Life*, one of his last pictures in his golden allegorical style, won first prize in Rome. The painting shows Death, pictured as the Grim Reaper to the side of the painting, staring at a mass of bodies in repose. These various individuals represent the cycle of life – the different ages of the human race – and in this image Klimt seems to be acknowledging that while death might take individuals, it cannot ever expect to wipe out the whole of humanity. In 1915, in response to his awareness of the work of European artists, and in particular Henri Matisse, Klimt reworked the painting, changing the background from gold to dark blue.

Change was in the air generally as many of Klimt's friends left to live abroad, including, in 1910, Oskar Kokoschka. Klimt stayed in Vienna but became increasingly isolated. Around this time he started to make an annual trip to a spa in Salzburg as a means of counterbalancing his ever-present tendency towards depression. Although it is

Death and Life, 1915. *Klimt first painted this work in 1908 and then overpainted the gold background with dark blue seven years later. This was most likely in response to his growing awareness of the work of other European painters whom he much admired.*

true that his work picked up on some of the stylistic changes going on in Europe, he did not fully embrace one particular style or radically depart from his previous subject matter.

*Lady with Hat and Feather Boa* (1909) and *Woman in Black Feather Hat* (1910) show the strong if temporary influence of Toulouse-Lautrec. Compare both these with Klimt's previous portraits of society ladies, as well as the femmes fatales. The composition is altogether simpler and less fussy. Gone are the white, wispy dresses and the proud but vacant look staring beyond the portrait. In place of the gold there's a preponderance of black – but black used to judicious effect. In *Lady with Hat and Feather Boa*, we can only partly see the unidentified woman's face and hair because they are covered by her hat and coat and further framed by the black-blue tones of the night sky. Behind her head, streaks and daubs of paint provide a hastily composed view of Paris, which Klimt might well have seen for himself on a night out. In the model's costume and pose, *The Black Feather Hat* more directly resembles a painting by Toulouse-Lautrec, while also making use of a restrained palette and pared down composition, which serves to heighten the pensive expression of the red-haired model.

No sooner had Klimt seemingly settled on a new style than he changed it to something else. Perhaps sensing that the femmes fatales had been his strongest suit, or calling card, he looked at ways of transforming this particular style into something less intimidating and something he felt would have a more universal appeal. Through Emilie Flöge, clothes and fashion

Woman in Black Feather Hat, *1910. In this work, influenced by Toulouse-Lautrec, Klimt appears to be turning away from his decorative style in a search for a new level of psychological intensity.*

Lady with Hat and Feather Boa, 1909. *The redheaded model
for this work is thought to be the same as the one for* Woman
in Black Feather Hat.

had always played a large part in Klimt's work and, for the later portraits, he brought together a startling and riotous amount of dresses, hats, flowers, fabrics and other decorative accessories to dress his models.

The portrait of *Mäda Primavesi* (1912–13) is an example of this new tendency in Klimt's work. Mäda is the daughter of one of Klimt's wealthiest patrons, the industrialist and banker Otto Primavesi and the actress Eugenia Primavesi. Nine-year-old Mäda stands with feet squarely apart, staring out of the canvas. Her intense, knowing stare makes her look older than her years, but the decorations attached to her hair and dress,

Mäda Primavesi, *1912–13. Mäda was the nine-year-old daughter of Otto Primavesi, one of Klimt's most important patrons. Primavesi's wife, Eugenia, sat for Klimt the following year.*

Portrait of Adele Bloch-Bauer II, *1912. The two commissioned portraits of Adele Bloch-Bauer reveal important differences. In this the second one, Adele stands full-frontal – her body merged into the vivid background filled with decorative motifs.*

and festooned around the room, have the effect of making her look younger. The colours in this portrait are a new departure for Klimt – lilac, emerald, lemon and icy blue – while the brushwork is generally freer and the decorative objects often of an indeterminate origin, although no less appealing because of that. Not long after, Klimt also painted Mäda's mother, Eugenia (c.1913), creating another intensely bright and patterned work in which the patchwork of patterns on her dress is almost merged into the mosaic-like background. In 1912, Klimt painted a second portrait of Adele Bloch-Bauer. Adele was only one of a couple of sitters who sat for Klimt twice. In this portrait her face with its faraway eyes and slightly open mouth closely resembles the earlier, infamous portrait of 1907. Klimt had earlier managed to capture the strong face of this tall, dark-haired beauty when he used her as his model for *Judith I* (1901) and *Judith II* (1909). In this decorative second portrait, there is an absence of gold. Adele stands erect, uncompromising, the waves of her gown cascading to the ground. Almost architectural, her dress is divided into sections, and a large circular hat frames her face. The background to the work is highly decorative – divided by colour into further sections that contain a profusion of floral motifs

Above left: Portrait of Elisabeth Baroness Bachofen-Echt, *1914. Elisabeth was the daughter of Klimt's patrons the Lederers and this painting was commissioned for her wedding. Her white dress is set against a background of colourful Japanese-inspired motifs.*

Portrait of Friederike Maria Beer, *1916. Friederike Maria Beer commissioned this portrait from Klimt directly. In it she wears a dress that she bought from the Wiener Werkstätte with material that Klimt hand-painted with spiral and eye motifs.*

and a range of ornamental objects. Bright colour and bold pattern suggest the influence of Matisse as well as Japanese woodcuts. Klimt was not alone in his appreciation of Japanese woodcuts. Many of the French Impressionists were also drawn to them and made similar use of 'a bird's-eye view', looking down at their subject from above, when planning the composition of their paintings. The Japanese influence is particularly clear in Klimt's later portraits such as *Portrait of Baroness Elisabeth Bachofen-Echt* (1914) and *Portrait of Friederike Maria Beer* (1916), where figures and objects surround the central figures who are depicted in highly patterned kimono style gowns. *The Virgin* (1912–13) suggests a return to the tangled compositions of earlier allegories. In an exotic pyramid of flowers and patterns, a young virgin dozes amid the writhing pale limbs of other young women. The colour is pure and bright and the brushstrokes thick and loose. The late allegories, like the earlier ones, do not contain a straightforward narrative and some of their meaning was lost on Klimt's contemporaries. What is clear here is Klimt's desire to evoke an entirely female world in which various states of pleasurable being such as desire and contentment are foregrounded. The feminine is consciously evoked through circular symbols, including the moon, the spiral and the shell.

The Virgin, *1912–13. To Klimt this allegorical vision of seven slumbering women entwined with flowers and a riot of patterns seems to represent a state of sexual expectation of awakening.*

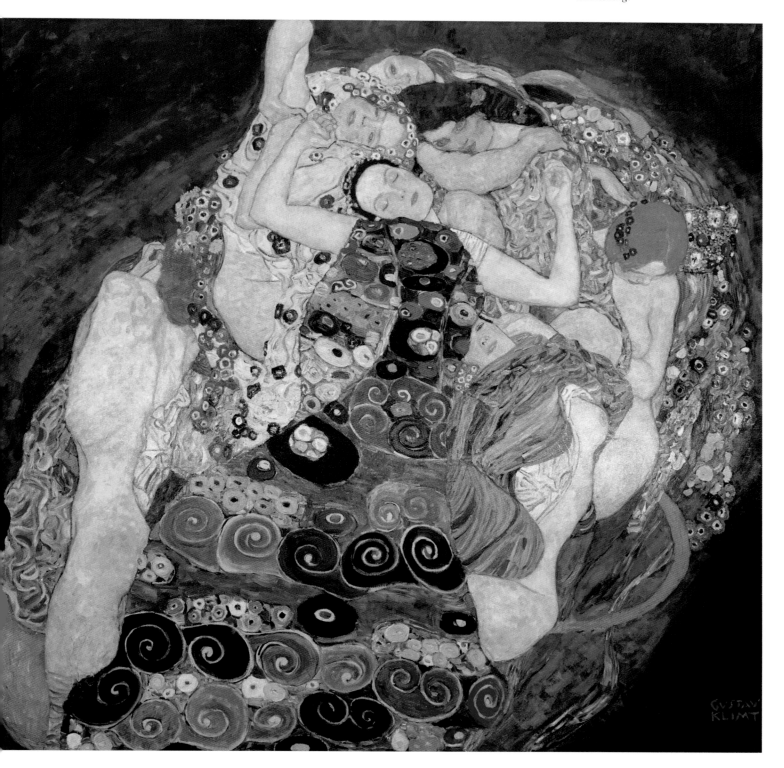

This new style of work, with its profusion of floral motifs and Oriental influences, proved highly successful: Klimt was once more a fashionable artist whose work was much in demand. As some critics have identified, however, this development of his femmes fatales portraits, in which the subjects themselves resemble giant dolls trapped, in a box is faintly disturbing. In neutralizing the dangerous vamp or siren, has Klimt started to infantilize his women instead?

In the last part of his life, Klimt retreated to his studio and garden as well as spending holidays on Lake Attersee at the Flöge family home. His wealthy patrons remained loyal to him and he continued to receive commissions. There was generally a waiting list for his

*Garden Path with Chickens, 1916. It is interesting to compare this painting with chickens to the earlier* After the Rain *(see page 61). The soft fluffiness of the earlier work has been replaced by an altogether bleaker, more sombre vision.*

portraits. Meanwhile, the Vienna he knew and loved was beginning to crumble around him. Events came to a head when Archduke Franz Ferdinand – Emperor Franz Joseph's heir – and his wife Sophie were shot dead in Serbia in 1914. A month later, Austria-Hungary declared war on Serbia, a move that had the calamitous effect of starting World War I.

The turmoil is reflected in Klimt's later work. Though his portraits show a riot of colour and pattern, the landscapes that he was painting in the corresponding years (between 1915 and 1918) show a move towards a more sombre palette and an altogether darker and more intense mood. In *Garden Path with Chickens* (1916), for example, the fluffy white chickens of the earlier similarly composed *After the Rain* have given way to a sharply delineated pair of black hens. The surrounding landscape is darker and more brooding, the vegetation stands upright by the side of the path, like soldiers forming a guard of honour. These landscapes are probably more reflective of Klimt's inner, private life than the portrait and the figure paintings, and could indicate his depressed state of mind following the grim reality of the outbreak of war in 1914 and the death of his mother in 1915. Klimt had taken on responsibility for his mother as a young man and she was a major influence on him all his life.

Women and eroticism were Klimt's all-encompassing themes and he continued to develop this aspect of his work right up until his death. *The Girlfriends* (1916–17) with its depiction of two female lovers – one clothed, one naked – is an example of Klimt's interest in depicting acts or moments of great sensuality. Infused with gorgeous red colour and filled with birds and flowers, it is perfectly possible to appreciate this painting on a purely aesthetic level. At the same time, while far from crude or vulgar, Klimt's ready enthusiasm for this type of work can seem a little prurient, even voyeuristic to contemporary eyes.

The Girlfriends, *1916–17. Many of the late works lie somewhere between portrait and allegory. These women appear to be a lesbian couple, but we are not given any further clues to their identity or the story behind the painting.*

# KLIMT'S DRAWINGS

Undeniably Klimt was a great draughtsman and throughout his career he was obsessed with drawing, often building up piles of drawings on his studio floor. He drew not only to make preparatory sketches for paintings, but also because he saw them as an essential part of his daily routine to keep his art practice alive and his hand flowing freely. At first, he worked on cheap materials such as chalk on wrapping paper, but in the later part of his career he worked on Japanese paper in pencil, sometimes introducing colour.

Klimt was a planner and when it came to his portraits and paintings, in particular his commissioned work, he did not leave anything to chance. For his *Portrait of Adele Bloch-Bauer I* alone, he made around 100 drawings. The sketches he made for the *Beethoven Frieze* and the *Stoclet Frieze* reveal some of the compositional experiments he made in advance of executing the work. Some of his later drawings are also preparatory sketches that he made for portraits, including several rapid line drawings of heads, feet and clothes that he made of Baroness Elisabeth Bachofen-Echt, and Friederike Maria Beer in 1916. Klimt did not leave behind any drawings of landscapes – if he did work on sketches for his paintings, which seems reasonable and quite possible, these did not survive,

Study for Portrait of Adele Bloch-Bauer I, *1903. In this study of Adele Bloch-Bauer rapidly composed in charcoal, Klimt notes the intricate details of her dress.*

Lust. *Study for* Beethoven Frieze, *c. 1902. In this study of a reclining nude, Klimt's model is typically self-absorbed – appearing here to be staring at her thumb.*

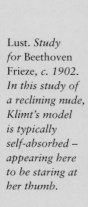

Nude; Halbakt, *1913. In many of
Klimt's erotic drawings, his models
appear half dressed. The artist is able
to conjure up the quality of flesh and
the texture of material with a spare,
casual use of line.*

Most of his later drawings were of the
female nude – mostly of a woman alone,
frequently in erotic poses. Sometimes,
the models are partially clothed, adding
another seductive element to the intimacy
of their pose. In most drawings they appear
unabashed, curling up or stretching out
sleepily as they lounge about. There is a
real tension in these drawings between
what is revealed and what remains hidden.
At times the intimate relationship between
the model and the artist is so apparent
that the viewer feels compromised and
is made to feel like a voyeur. The female
subjects are anonymous and passive – we
are made aware of the artist's gaze and
his manipulation of the situation. Yet the
models themselves have the same mixture
of haughtiness, distance and sangfroid that
we see in the paintings of femmes fatales,
which helps to suggest that they are the
ones who have real control here.

Aside from their explicitness, however,
the drawings themselves are incredible
studies of the female form, effortlessly done
and beautifully positioned on the page. In
some of the later drawings, the scribble
of lines just dances across the page. These
free, fluid studies of women have a direct
quality of line and gesture that make them
some of Klimt's best work.

Klimt rarely exhibited his erotic
drawings, realizing that they were too
much for even *fin-de-siècle* Vienna to
handle. In 1918, the year of his death,
the art dealer Gustav Nebehay produced
an exhibition of some of these works.
More than 3000 of Klimt's drawings have
survived, although they are rarely put on
public display. This is partly down to their
frank subject matter and partly because
many of them are in the hands of private
collectors.

Portrait of
Johanna Staude,
*1917–18. This
portrait was
unfinished at the
time of Klimt's
death from a
stroke in February
1918. How much
further would
Klimt have been
tempted to work
on it?*

*Baby (Cradle), 1917–18. An arresting image because of the dramatic foreshortening, it seems ironic that one of Klimt's last paintings was of a baby in a cradle.*

Pictures of Klimt's studio taken towards the end of his life show some of the unfinished pieces he was working on before he died. These revealed that he worked on several canvases at one time. *Portrait of Johanna Staude* (1917–18) shows a closer head and shoulders view of his model, who wears a patterned blue and purple coat with a black fur collar. Her stare is uncompromising and there is relatively little in the way of decoration. Would Klimt have been tempted to adorn the background had he lived? *The Bride*, another unfinished work from the same period, shows a heap of female bodies representing various erotic states such as desire and ecstasy. As such it forms a narrative companion to Klimt's work *The Virgin* – indeed, two of the faces in this work are very similar to a couple in this earlier work. There is also – unusually in Klimt's allegorical work – a man. It is a bird's-eye view seen from above, inspired by the Japanese art that Klimt was drawn to and collected.

*Baby (Cradle)* is another extraordinary unfinished image. This is not an allegorical painting but rather a powerful depiction of a baby, whose tiny head appears in foreshortening above its blanket – a technicolour mountain of undulating patterns. Loosely handled and full of movement and life, it seems ironic that this expressive work should be one of Klimt's last.

Just 10 months before the cessation of the war in 1918, Klimt had a stroke that paralyzed him on his right side. He was 55. He asked for Emilie, who came to be with him at his bedside, but he became sick with pneumonia and influenza and died on 6 February.

*Gustav Klimt's funeral took place on 9 February 1918 at the Hietzing Cemetery in Vienna.*

## KLIMT'S LEGACY AND INFLUENCE

Klimt is one of the most reproduced artists in the world, so it might seem churlish to say that his influence is limited. But he is a representative of a particular time and place that is now dead and buried. There has been no other artist quite like Klimt. His work – and his golden allegorical paintings in particular – belongs to an era of unimaginable luxury and excess, which we can no longer conjure up, let alone fathom. Overtaken by the horror of World War I, Klimt's art appears outdated and isolated.

Even in his own time Klimt seems out of place. All the great artists who were his contemporaries appear more modern, doing much more to create or further the styles and movements of their particular day, whether that is Expressionists like Munch,

The Cardinal and the Nun (Caress), Egon Schiele, 1912. *In repainting some of Klimt's themes, in this case* The Kiss, *Schiele adopts a much darker even violent approach.*

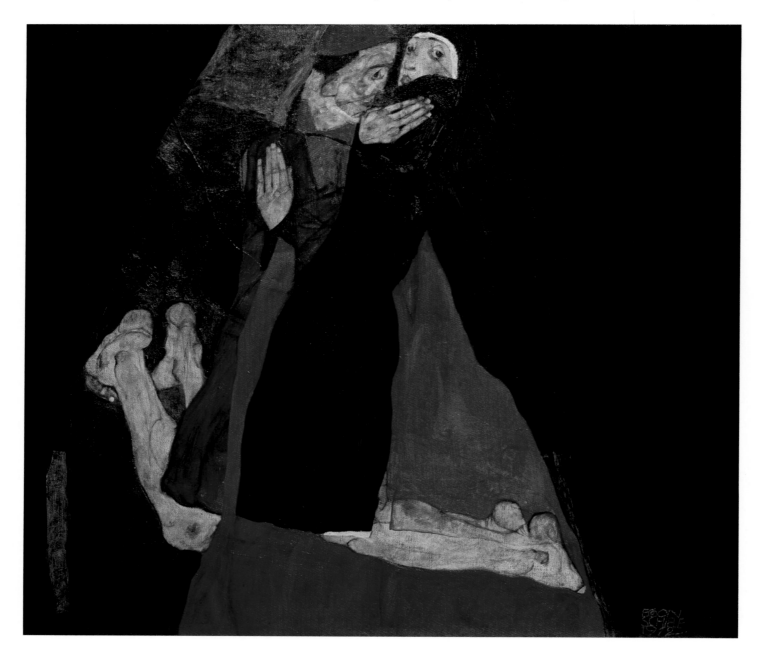

Impressionists like Cézanne, or abstract artists like Kandinsky. In 1907, just as Klimt was working on *Portrait of Adele Bloch-Bauer I*, his golden bejewelled Egyptian queen, Picasso was creating *Les Demoiselles d'Avignon*, his groundbreaking cubist-inspired work with its five working girls.

And yet there is so much to admire about Klimt. His skills as a draughtsman are truly remarkable and his direct, expressive studies of the female form go beyond their sensual or erotic subject matter to reveal an astounding, almost casual ease with line, perspective and mark making.

His landscapes are also unique. Even today it is hard to find an artist whose vision comes close to Klimt's. Despite the extraordinary level of detail – showing us every leaf and every twig – the world that he conjures up is far from naturalistic. It is an hermetically sealed world, and rather than offering us a window onto the world, Klimt puts up a wall through which we cannot enter. This wall is made up of myriad little parts which, like the view through a kaleidoscope, suddenly shift and split into further tiny pieces. The view he offers is singular, untouched by time, yet knowable in a way that recalls dreams which are at once lurid, enchanting and faintly disturbing.

Although no school followed him, he did – for a while, at least – have disciples in Oskar Kokoschka and Egon Schiele. The latter is especially interesting in that it is a case where the pupil, Schiele, overtakes his master in terms of reach and influence.

Around 1911, Schiele began to repaint some of Klimt's themes. With its lovers bound tightly together, *Cardinal and Nun (The Caress)* is clearly based on Klimt's *The Kiss*. The initial intention might have been to pay homage to his master, but Schiele's portrayal of an illicit relationship between two religious figures appears to be both a parody and criticism of his master's work. Furthermore, Schiele appears to be using this subject matter to allude to events and circumstances in his own life.

In Schiele's much darker and intense version, the couple are pitted against each other, in an embrace that looks far from tender and is clearly meant to be seen as a violation of moral codes. Themes of violence and sexual power underscore the image. The triangular composition of the painting seems to suggest a blasphemous reference to the Trinity. The couple's facial expressions display a mix of confusion, fear and secrecy and their naked legs are bent and tense. In a predominantly black painting, the cardinal's bright red cape stands out, a literal red flag.

It appears that Schiele not only wishes to provoke but also hint at issues beyond the picture frame. This painting directly or indirectly relates to events in his own life: during this same year, he was arrested for aiding a 13-year-old girl escape from her father to return to her grandmother.

Schiele made a drawing of Klimt in the morgue of Vienna's General Hospital just after he died. Entitled *The Dead Klimt*, the drawing shows a tiny shrunken head floating in the top half of the paper, with hollowed eyes and no familiar beard. Before the end of the year Schiele would be dead too – also a victim of influenza that swept through Vienna.

Klimt had mentored Schiele in the early part of his career, but by 1912 Schiele was breaking away and finding his own artistic language. Anguish and isolation are the characteristic features of Schiele's style – bodies are often emaciated and vulnerable, a physical fragility and expressiveness that seems far away from the myths and allegories of Klimt's golden world.

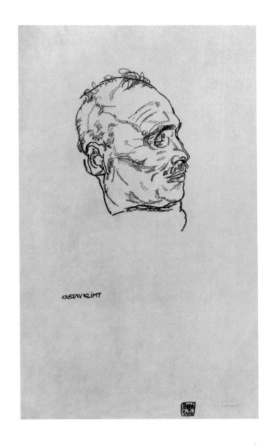

Head of the Dead Gustav Klimt, *Egon Schiele, 1918. Schiele drew this portrait of Klimt in the mortuary of Vienna's General Hospital.*

# TIMELINE

## 1860s

**'62** Gustav Klimt born in Baumgarten.

## 1870s

**'76** Enters the Kunstgewerbeschule (Vienna School of Arts and Crafts), where he studies for seven years.

**'77** Gustav's brother, Ernst and their friend Franz Matsch (1861–1942) also enrol in the school.

**'79** Work on decorations for *Festzug*, the pageant celebrating Emperor Franz Joseph's silver wedding. Forms Künstler–Compagnie (Painters' Company).

## 1880s

**'80** The Company create four decorative ceiling paintings for the Palais Sturany in Vienna.

**'84** Gustav's hero Hans Makart dies an early death aged 44.

**'85** The Painters' Company work on a scheme for the Villa Hermes (Hermesvilla), Emperor Franz Joseph's country residence near Vienna.

**'86** The Painters' Company work on the interior of the Burgtheater, the replacement for the old theatre in Vienna.

**'88** Klimt receives the Emperor's Golden Cross of Honour for his contributions to the Burgtheater murals.

## 1890s

**'90** The Painter's Company work on the newly built Kunsthistorisches (Museum of Art History) in Vienna. A separate painting, *Auditorium in the Old Burgtheater*, 1888, receives the Imperial Award.

**'91** Klimt becomes a member of the co-operative Austrian Artists' Society, the traditional Viennese forum for artists.

**'92** Klimt's father and brother Ernst die.

**'94** Klimt and Matsch commissioned to produce four decorative panels in the great hall of the University of Vienna.

**'95** Klimt sends work to the publisher Martin Gerlach for *Allegories and Emblems*.

**'97** Klimt founds the Vienna Seccession and is elected its President. Spends summer with companion Emilie Flöge in the region of Kammer on the Attersee.

**'98** First Secession exhibition. Founding of journal *Ver Sacrum*. Paints *Portrait of Sonja Knips* and *Pallas Athene*.

**'99** Completes decoration of Dumba Palace Music Room. Paints *Music II* and *Schubert at the Piano*.

## 1900s

**'00** Klimt's rejected Secession painting *Philosophy* awarded gold medal in Paris.

**'01** Klimt's painting *Medicine* causes further outrage at Seccession exhibition. Paints *Judith* and the *Head of Holofernes*.

**'02** Meets Auguste Rodin, who admires Klimt's *Beethoven Frieze* in Secession building.

**'03** Visits Ravenna in Italy and sees the Byzantine mosaics. Beginning of the Golden Phase. Paints *Jurisprudence*.

**'04** Draws plans for wall mosaics for the Palais Stoclet in Brussels. Paints *Water Serpents*.

**'05** Klimt and friends leave the Secession. Paints *The Three Ages of Woman*.

**'07** Start of friendship with Egon Schiele. Paints *Danaë* and Adele Bloch-Bauer.

**'08** Paints *The Kiss*. Sixteen paintings shown at the Kunstschau, Vienna.

**'09** Beginning of work on *Stoclet Frieze*. Paints *Judith II*.

## 1910s

**'10** Success at 9th Venice Biennale.

**'11** *Death and Life* painting wins first prize in Rome.

**'15** Reworks *Death and Life*, painting over the gold background.

**'15** Death of his mother.

**'16** Paints *The Girlfriends*. Death of Emperor Franz Joseph.

**'17** Starts work on *The Bride*. Begins *Baby (Cradle)* (unfinished).

**'18** Klimt has a stroke and dies. Numerous unfinished works. End of the Habsburg Empire.

## FURTHER INFORMATION

Gill, D. M., *Klimt (Discovering Art: The Life, Times and Work of the World's Greatest Artists series)*, Brockhampton Press, London, 1996

Hodge, Susie, *Gustav Klimt: Masterpieces of Art*, Flame Tree Publishing, London, 2014

Kerrigan, Michael, *Gustav Klimt: Art Nouveau and the Vienna Secessionists*, Flame Tree Publishing, London, 2015

Natter, Tobias G. & Grunenberg, Christoph (ed.), *Gustav Klimt – Painting, Design and Modern Life*, Tate Publishing, London, 2008

Néret, Gilles, *Klimt, 1862–1918*, Taschen, Cologne & London, 2007

di Stefano, Eva, *Gustav Klimt: Art Nouveau Visionary*, Sterling Publishing, New York, 2008

Whitford, Frank, *Klimt*, Thames & Hudson, London, 1990

## WEBSITES

Belvedere Museum, Vienna – belvedere.at
Burgtheater – burgtheater.at
klimt.com
Kunsthistoriches Museum – khm.at
Leopold Museum, Vienna – leopoldmuseum.org
Neue Galerie – neuegalerie.org
Secession Building – secession.at
theartstory.org

# LIST OF ILLUSTRATIONS

## INDEX